TOMART's
illustrated
DISNEYANA
catalog and price guide
VOLUME TWO

by Tom Tumbusch

Edited by Bob and Claire Raymond

Consultant David R. Smith, Archivist
Walt Disney Productions

Color Photography by Tom Schwartz

TOMART PUBLICATIONS
division of Tomart Corporation
Dayton, Ohio

To Bob and Claire Raymond
for their help on preparing this 3-volume guide and their many contribu-
tions to the study and collection of Disneyana.

ACKNOWLEDGEMENTS

These books have not been a small undertaking. Many people have helped. Some made major contributions to this extensive DISNEYANA research project. Every bit of information, photocopy, or actual photo helped make the books a little better. I would like to thank these individuals plus the many collectors and dealers who permitted me to photograph their Disneyana items. Special thanks go to Bob Lesser, Harvey and Jan Kamins, Richard Kamins, Ted Hake, Harry Hall, Jim Silva, Bob Coup, John Koukoutsakis, Joe Sarno, Bill Joppeck, Dave and Elaine Hughes, Jerry and Mona Cook, Bruce and Linda Cervon, Donna and Keith Kaonis, Bernie Shine, Morris Hamasaki, Phil Ellis and Carol, Ed and Elaine Levin, Bob Molinari, Don and Dee Toms, Evie Wilson, Jean Toll, Charles Sexton, Karl Price, Stan Pawlowski, Kim and Julie McEuen, Ray Walsh, Dennis Mathiason, Roger Le Roque, Nick Farago, Greg Shelton, George McIntyre, Von Crabill and George Hagenauer for their help . . . and to Virginia Gann for caring so many years for her Borgfeldt ducks.

For their moral support and guidance outside the field of Disneyana I am deeply indebted to Stan Freedman, Marilyn Scott, Pete Trohatos, Kirk Febus, Dave Gross, George Might, Karen Morgan, and Rebecca Trissel.

My daughter Amy provided assistance in many ways, particularly in assembling and filing the thousands of bits of data, plus assistance in photographing her stuffed characters and dolls, and help with the final artwork.

A special thanks also to Rick Lenhard and his crew at Boldruler Typesetters for excellent service and cooperation in providing the typography. Central Printing in Dayton and Carpenter Lithographers in Springfield, Ohio printed the three volumes. Production help thanks are also in order for Tom Vukovic and his staff at CompuColor and to Brock Hull at Hull Paper Co.

Everyone who enjoys the 60 pages of color photography in the three volumes can thank Tom Schwartz and his assistant, Fred Boomer, for over six months of work setting up and photographing all the items shown in color.

And to the editors — collectors Bob and Claire Raymond, and Dave Smith, Archivist, Walt Disney Productions and Paula Sigman, Assistant Archivist — for all the time they spent reviewing, correcting, and otherwise improving the manuscript, I extend my personal gratitude.

Lastly it's a proud father who thanks his 16 year old son, Thomas N., for entering everything into an Atari 800 computer, for many rewrites, and a large part of the typesetting job. We stuck it out together.

Tom Tumbusch
November, 1985

The Tomart Illustrated DISNEYANA Catalog and Price Guide will be updated on a regular basis. If you wish to be notified when the supplements become available, send a self-addressed stamped envelope to Tomart Publications, P. O. Box 2102, Dayton, OH 45429.

Library of Congress Catalog Card Number: 85-51198

ISBN: 0-914293-01-8

Printed in U.S.A.

Mickey Mouse *and his creator* Walt Disney

Newspaper publicity photo and caption from 1932.

WALT DISNEY'S "SNOW WHITE AND THE SEVEN DWARFS"

Snow White and the Seven Dwarfs *fan card.*

In Volume One of *Tomart's Illustrated DISNEYANA Catalog* and *Price Guide* information on collecting Disneyana, clubs, publications, antique toy shows, auctions, and similar source data was presented. *The Disney Time Line* traced the history of Walt Disney and his various companies from his first art lessons in 1915 through *Fantasia* in 1940. Covered were his early failures and disappointments, his eventual success, plus various character developments useful in dating Disneyana, and the first three animated features — *Snow White and the Seven Dwarfs, Pinocchio,* and *Fantasia.*

The Disney Time Line continues as Walt Disney's American dream was about to be interrupted by World War II.

Brave Little Tailor

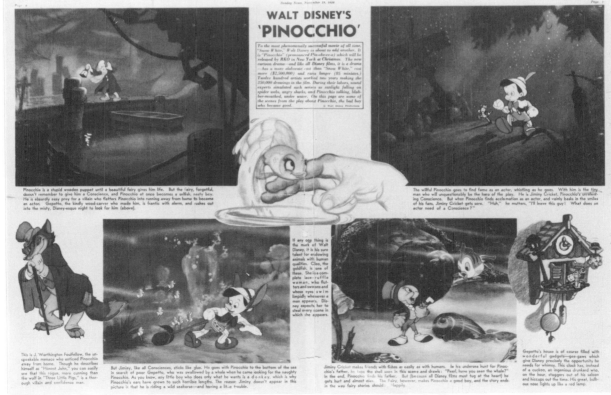

Pinocchio *publicity article from Nov 19, 1939* New York Sunday News.

Fantasia movie program (1940). Detail of Hyacinth Hippo and Ben Ali Gator dancing.

1941

Even though there were some live takes of Leopold Stokowski in *Fantasia, The Reluctant Dragon* (June 20) is considered Disney's first film to rely on live action to carry most of the story. The production is a tour of the Disney Studio. Walt and many other Studio regulars took part. In the course of seeing the studio at work, Robert Benchley sees four animated shorts unreeled: *Casey Jr., Baby Weems, How to Ride a Horse* (Goofy) and *The Reluctant Dragon.*

The low budget *Reluctant Dragon* wasn't enough to recover the losses *Fantasia* posted. So *Dumbo* (Oct 23) was designed to bolster studio finances. It is one of the shortest Disney animated features and the only one to cost less than $1 million

to produce. Characters of note included: Dumbo, Mr. Stork, Timothy Mouse, Casey Jr. and the Crows who first taught an elephant to fly.

Eighteen cartoons were released. A Pluto cartoon won an Academy Award — *Lend a Paw*, while Mickey and Minnie shined in *The Nifty Nineties* and a color remake of *The Orphan's Benefit.* Mickey appeared with dimensional ears for a brief time during this period — in cartoons and on a very few Disneyana items. *Truant Officer Donald* led the slate of eight Duck cartoons. Pluto did a total of four, Mickey and Goofy each did three.

The bombing of Pearl Harbor on Dec 7 had an immediate impact on the studio and Disneyana. The military took over the sound stage for several months to use as a repair facility. Material shortages developed and, of course, Japanese-produced Disneyana came to an abrupt halt.

No more Kay Kamen merchandise catalogs were produced until 1947.

The Victory March book depicted Disney villains as the enemy and promoted the sale of War Bonds to children (left). Detail from 1942 wall plaque, one of the few Disneyana items to show Mickey Mouse with dimensional ears (right).

1942

The Disney Studio supported the war effort, savings bond drives, and USO entertainment activities. Disney artists designed over a thousand military insignias and made scores of animated training films. *Bambi* premiered August 13 and went into general release on the 21st. The main characters were Aunt Ena, Bambi's Mother, Bambi, Faline, Friend Owl, Ronno, Flower, and Thumper. Merchandising on the film was restrained due to the war. Still, *Bambi* has endured as a popular Disneyana character ever since.

Dell Full Color Comic No.9 featured "Donald Duck Finds Pirate Gold", the first to feature the unique comic art talent of Carl Barks. Barks' mastery of simple black lines communicated greater character depth and expression than most other artists. Donald's explosive character was a perfect foil for Barks, who often wrote the stories as well. In future years, he created new characters, including Gladstone Gander, Grandma Duck, and Uncle Scrooge. To add frosting on the cake, most Barks art has a distinctive eye treatment that quickly identifies his work.

Several of the 19 cartoons released had war themes: *Donald Gets Drafted, The Army Mascot* (Pluto), *Donald's Garden,*

4

A re-release ad for the 1942 animated classic, Bambi.

The 1939 color re-make of The Ugly Duckling was the last film in the Silly Symphony series. As a crowning touch it won an Academy Award

"Donald Duck Finds Pirate Gold", the first of many Carl Barks comic books.

The Disney Studio was just building up momentum when the U. S. was pulled into World War II. A rapid shift in plans found the animators turning out military training films.

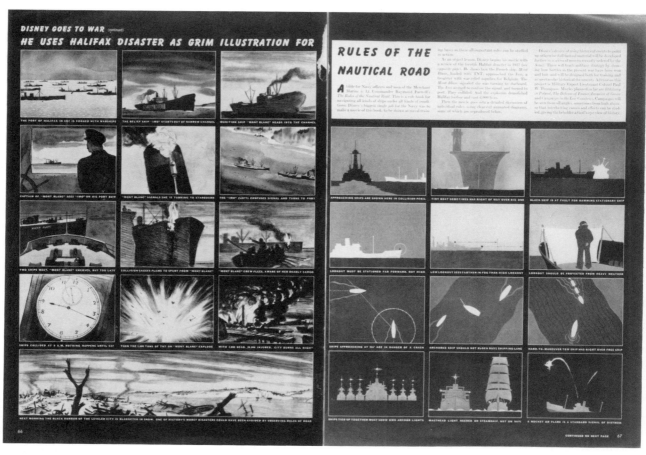

Rules of the Nautical Road *and* Stop That Tank *were just two of the many training films the Disney Studio produced in support of the war effort.*

Rounded faces of characters as they appeared in Mickey's Birthday Party. *No new Mickey cartoons were released from 1943 until 1947.*

and *The Vanishing Private*. Mickey's fifteenth birthday was celebrated in *Mickey's Birthday Party*. The cartoon breakdown was Donald (8), Pluto (5), Goofy (4), and Mickey (2). Mickey had become "Mr. Nice Guy" in response to his respected worldwide reputation. Any hint of a bad example would bring a flood of letters to the Studio.

1943

It must have been an interesting year at the Studio. Disney's appeal to South American countries to replace lost revenues from war torn Europe was a great success. Major films and cartoons continued to support the war effort. It also seemed to be a period of philosophical questioning and some interesting films were the result.

Saludos Amigos (Hello Friends) used footage of Walt's tour of South America to patch together four animated shorts: *Lake Titicaca* (with Donald Duck), *Pedro* (a young airmail plane on his first solo flight through treacherous, but beautiful mountains), *El Gaucho Goofy,* and *Aquarela do Brazil* (Watercolor of Brazil). The Feb 6 release introduced Pedro and Joe Carioca.

Sheet music from Saludos Amigos *and* Der Fuehrer's Face.

Training film production exposed Walt to many military concepts and theories. He became convinced the U.S. needed to develop long range strategic bombing capability (not a popular idea at the Pentagon) and produced *Victory Through Air Power* (July 17) to factually state the case.

Donald starred in the Academy Award-winning *Der Fuehrer's Face, Fall Out-Fall In,* and *The Old Army Game*. Chip 'n' Dale made their debut in *Private Pluto*, but weren't named until 1947. Goofy did *Victory Vehicles*. Two characters from an animated feature tried a solo act in *Figaro and Cleo*, and for the first time since 1928, there wasn't a new Mickey Mouse cartoon. There were, however, three rather heavy shorts — *Education for Death* featuring Germania, Hans, and Hitler; *Reason and Emotion;* and *Chicken Little* with Cocky Locky, Ducky Lucky, Foxey Loxey, Goosey Loosey, Henny Penny, and Turkey Lurkey all worrying about the sky falling.

The Gremlins, curious little characters (Gremlins, Fifinellas, and Widgets) that plague aviators, were the subject of an abandoned 1943 project. The film is known to Disneyana collectors due to a Random House book licensed for publicity.

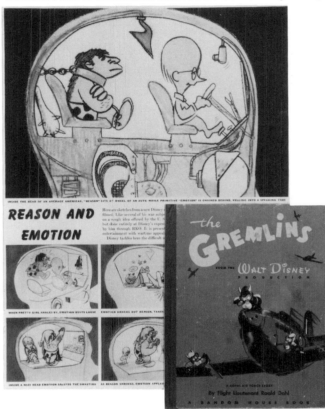

Storyboard drawings from Reason and Emotion *as they appeared in an unidentified magazine article along with the Random House book featuring the never produced story for* The Gremlins.

Postal zones first came into effect this year. Any original Disneyana on which a postal zone appears (i.e. New York 1, N.Y.) was produced between 1943 and 1964.

1944

The Studio was deeply involved in the war effort. Only twelve shorts were released. There were no features of note. On June 6, Mickey Mouse was used as the code word when Allied Forces landed on the occupied French coast in the battle that eventually led to victory in Europe. *Donald's Trombone Trouble* and Goofy's *How to Play Football* represented the better films ... and for the second straight year, there were no new Mickey cartoons.

On the surface it didn't appear much was happening. However, a 1944 Simon and Schuster edition revealed several projects were already in development. Titled "*Surprise Pack-*

age", it provided the first look at Disney's Brer Rabbit, *Alice in Wonderland, Peter Pan, Adventures of Mr. Toad, Lady and the Tramp,* and several characters that were included in later feature films.

1945

The Three Caballeros (Feb 3) provided signs Disney was alive and well. This time it was Donald visiting the lower Americas publicizing their natural beauty. Animated segments were *The Cold-Blooded Penguin, The Flying Gauchito* and the brilliantly combined live action/animation of Donald and Joe Carioca's tour of various countries and their meeting Panchito — culminating in the razzle dazzle *The Three Caballeros* animated sequence.

There were 15 shorts — one headlined Donald and Goofy, while Donald did six others and Goofy four. *The Legend of Coyote Rock* paced Pluto's four films. *Donald's Crime* was nominated for an Oscar and *Tiger Trouble* was possibly Goofy's best for the year.

The *Uncle Remus* color Sunday strip began Oct 14, and ran through Dec 31, 1972. Character merchandise income had declined throughout the war years due to shortages that restricted the production of typical licensed products. Food products, while rationed, still competed in an open market. Earlier efforts to develop this sort of revenue started to pay off. Donald Duck, due to his popularity, was almost always the endorsing character. A large variety of food and drink companies became licensees. When Disney became involved in television, new food licensing was discouraged to avoid conflicts with advertisers. A few licensees (such as Donald Duck Orange Juice) continue to the present.

1946

The return to peace time paved the way for lighter, happy films and a resurgence of Disneyana merchandise. *Make Mine Music* (Aug 15) was planned as a popular music counterpart to *Fantasia.* The ten animated shorts were: *A Rustic Ballad* with the Martins and the Coys; Tone Poem ("*Blue Bayou*"); A Jazz

(Right) Three sequences from Make Mine Music.

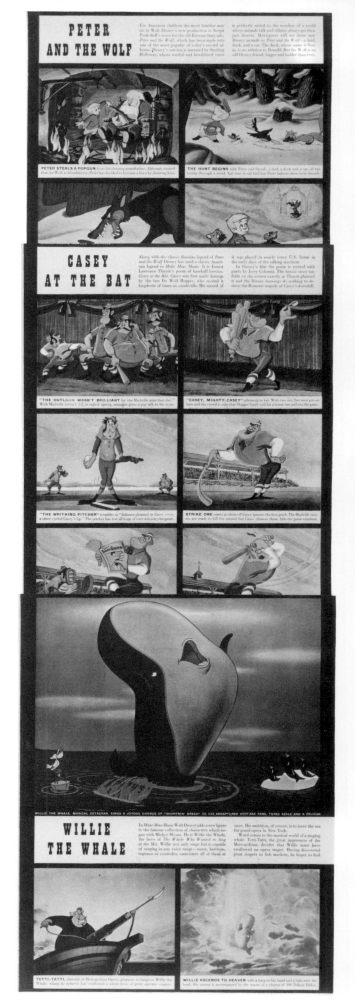

Interlude ("All the Cats Join In"); *A Ballad In Blue* ("Without You"); *A Musical Recitation (Casey at The Bat)*, Ball-ade Ballet ("Two Silhouettes"); *A Fairy Tale With Music (Peter and the Wolf); After You've Gone*, a surrealistic jazz sequence; *A Love Story* ("Johnny Fedora and Alice Blue Bonnet"); and *Opera Pathetique* with Willie the Whale doing several arias while realizing his fantasy on stage at the Met.

Brer Rabbit, Brer Fox, and Brer Bear came to life in *Song of the South* (Nov 12). "Zip-A-Dee-Doo-Dah" won an Oscar for best song, but the sheet music art ranks among the poorest designs. There were twelve cartoons along the same pattern of previous years.

Disneyana from Japan began to reappear. Items produced from 1946 to 1951 are often marked — Made in Occupied Japan.

Song of the South *fan card.*

1947

A new Kay Kamen merchandise catalog was issued, indicating character licensing had regained much of its pre-war strength.

Fun and Fancy Free (Sept 27) included two featurettes: *Bongo* and *Mickey and the Beanstalk* along with live action sequences of Edgar Bergen, Charlie McCarthy and Mortimer Snerd. *Mickey's Delayed Date* was the first Mickey cartoon since 1942. *Chip 'an' Dale* formally named the chipmunks.

Bongo and Lulubelle as featured on the Fun and Fancy Free *fan card.*

Fan card for Melody Time.

Pluto's Blue Note was another outstanding short of the 15 new ones released. Cartoons from the Disney library were also re-released for the first time.

1948

Melody Time (May 27), often acclaimed the best of the postwar musical short composites, featured *Little Toot, Johnny Appleseed, Once Upon A Wintertime, Bumble Boogie, Trees, Blame it on the Samba* (reuniting Donald Duck, Joe Carioca, and Panchito), and *Pecos Bill* (featuring the cowboy star, Roy Rogers).

Three for Breakfast, Mickey and the Seal and *Tea for Two Hundred* were the most notable of the 16 shorts released. Gladstone Gander first appeared in *Walt Disney Comics and Stories #88* — another product of Carl Barks.

The 1948-49 edition of Ice Capades introduced arena audiences to Disney costumed characters similar to the ones that would later inhabit Disneyland.

1949

So Dear To My Heart (Jan 19) introduced Danny, the little black lamb. *Seal Island* (May 4) was the first True-Life Adventure, a series of naturalist films that both educated and entertained. Originally two-reel shorts, later titles were made feature length. *Toy Tinkers* was nominated for an Academy Award over the other 14 cartoons released.

The major film of the year was *The Adventures of Ichabod and Mr. Toad* (Oct 5). Once again, Disney characters showed

Fan card for The Adventures of "Ichabod and Mr. Toad."

depth — the animation, real class. Respectively based on *The Legend of Sleepy Hollow* and *The Wind in the Willows*, the film produced little character merchandise. A puzzling situation in view of such grand characters as Ichabod Crane, Katrina Van Tassel, Brom Bones and the Headless Horseman astride Gunpowder. Fun-loving J. Thaddeus Toad, Winky and Cyril, along with Mole, Rat, and Mac Badger (the sensible keepers of Toad Hall) seemed also to offer some great opportunities.

Perhaps those opportunities were lost due to the untimely death of Kay Kamen, who, together with his wife, was killed in a European plane crash on October 29. Upon his death, the company established the Character Merchandising Division. The last Kay Kamen Merchandise Catalog (1949-50) had already been printed. Since that time, merchandise has been promoted in smaller mailers and catalogs, and in film press books.

Left side of a two page US Time ad showing the air-brushed style, boyish Mickey Mouse characteristic of the late 40's to early 50's.

1950

Cinderella, the first animated feature telling a single story, since *Bambi*, arrived on Feb 15. In addition to the age old characters of Cinderella, the Prince, stepmother and stepsisters, Disney added Gus, Jaq, and a handful of neatly dressed mice, Bruno the dog, and an obese, aptly named cat called Lucifer. The King and Grand Duke were also new characters. The Fairy Godmother was a delightful departure from the stock version. *Cinderella* was the most merchandised film since *Pinocchio*. *Treasure Island* (July 19), one of several live action films made in England to use cash restricted to the country, was a limited source of Disneyana.

Two press book photos from the 1950 Walt Disney release Cinderella.

Eighteen cartoons and the Oscar-winning *Beaver Valley* True-Life Adventure were released. Pluto was the major star with eight films headed by *Pluto's Heart Throb*. Donald appeared in six. Cartoons, at one time the total basis for character merchandise, were having less and less influence. The characters were no longer merchandised in relation to any particular film. Their personalities were established and the handwriting on the wall numbered the days for theatrical cartoon shorts.

TV was invented the same year as Mickey in 1928 — color TV in 1929. The depression slowed development, but the one-eyed marvel was impressively demonstrated at the 1939 New York World's Fair. The war prevented production. Post-war sets were few and expensive. Programming sparse. By 1948, there was a scramble for VHF licenses. Lower cost TV sets were in mass production by 1949. The new medium had a major impact on network radio and movie theaters by 1950. Movie theaters were being forced to cut expenses by eliminating newsreels and short subjects. Walt was cautious, but got a TV deal on his own terms.

The first Disney TV special — "One Hour In Wonderland" — aired Christmas Day at 4:00 pm to a huge audience — the largest ever at that time.

The Disney Time Line concludes in Volume Three of Tomart's Illustrated DISNEYANA Catalog and Price Guide.

IMPORTANT — Please read the explanation of dates and values on page 12. This statement is an intricate part of every date and value estimate in this three volume series.

These mean your biggest year in dolls

FOR the first time in the history of Mickey Mouse Dolls, this world famous character is dressed in costume. The incomparable popularity of Mickey Mouse plus the romance of cowboy chaps, sombrero, 'kerchief, lariat and pistols is scoring a hit and staging a real show in salesmanship. Mickey Clown is running a close second and the standard Mickey Mouse and Minnie Mouse Dolls are maintaining a volume heretofore unbelievable!

Write for full particulars

KNICKERBOCKER TOY CO.
Licensee
85 Fifth Avenue
New York, N. Y.

D6302

D6327

D6328

D6301

D6356   D6353   D6355   D6350   D6326   D6325

PLUTO THE PUP

DONALD DUCK

BIG BAD WOLF

D6351

ELMER ELEPHANT

ORPHAN KITTENS

ROBBER KITTEN

TOBY TORTOISE

MISS COTTONTAIL

D6352   D6336   D6335   D6337

D6354

11

At each classification there is a brief overview of the material covered, followed by item listings. Included is the best information currently available on manufacturers and the years licensed. THIS INFORMATION IS NOT ALL-INCLUSIVE AND ERRORS UNDOUBTEDLY EXIST. The information is most reliable for the years 1934-50 and from 1970 to 1984, although it might not be precise. In some cases the possible error is the listing of a year not licensed. More often it will be the absence of a year in which Disney products were made. In some cases a manufacturer's name appears under a classification even though none of its products are listed. The licensing records are sound, but the items have yet to be located and cataloged by the author.

Price range estimates are based on the experience of the author. In cases where sufficient trade experience is absent, best guesstimates are provided. Where a price range refers to different size items, the high end refers to the largest size. The greater the price spread, the more valuable a strictly mint item. Also, in the case of a wide price range, "fine" grade items are worth substantially less than the average or mid-price shown. If the price range shown is 10-100, the fine value is around 40 not 50 to 55.

This sometimes flawed information is provided in the belief that available data will lead to improved scholarship in the future. Any collectors or former Disney employees having printed data or dated Disneyana material that clarifies this information are encouraged to send photos of items or photocopies of printed material to Tom Tumbusch c/o Tomart Publications, P.O. Box 2102, Dayton, Ohio 45429.

D6370   D6371

D6393

D6370

D6340

D6325

DONALD DUCK

PLUTO THE PUP

ORPHAN KITTENS

ELMER ELEPHANT

ROBBER KITTEN

D6380   D6381   D6382

1935 Knickerbocker

D6325	Mickey w/composition shoes	35 - 250
D6326	Minnie w/composition shoes	35 - 250
D6327	Clown Mickey	75 - 800
D6328	Six-Gun Mickey, suede chaps	75 - 900

1936 Knickerbocker

D6335	Donald, composition	25 - 200
D6336	Two-Gun Mickey, tufted chaps	75 - 650
D6337	Western Minnie	50 - 350
D6340	Donald, stuffed, 2 sizes	50 - 650
D6341	Drum major Donald	50 - 500

1936 Krueger

D6350	Big Bad Wolf	25 - 75
D6351	Robber Kitten	25 - 75
D6352	Toby Tortoise	15 - 60
D6353	Elmer Elephant	20 - 65
D6354	3 Orphan Kittens, each	10 - 30
D6355	Donald Duck w/sailor hat	35 - 150
D6356	Pluto the Pup	25 - 75

1938 Snow White and the Seven Dwarfs

D6368	Alexander Snow White	50 - 350
D6369	Alexander Dwarfs, each	25 - 75
D6370	Ideal Snow White (3 sizes)	30 - 150
D6371	Ideal Dwarfs, each	20 - 150
D6374	Knickerbocker Snow White (3 sizes)	35 - 180
D6375	Knickerbocker Wicked Queen	40 - 200
D6376	Knickerbocker Dwarfs (2 sizes)	15 - 50

D6375

D6377

D6374

D6376

D6380

D6400

D6395   D6391   D6397

D6374

D6394

D6390   D6341

D6451   D6447   D6447   D6450

D6415   D6413   D6410

D6411   D6410   D6417

D6440

D6445

D6503   D6501   D6501

D6505

D6504

D6510

D6512   D6513

D6514   D6517

D6377	Knickerbocker Forest Animals (each)	10 - 45
D6380	Krueger Snow White (velvet or organdie)	30 - 150
D6381	Krueger Dwarfs (sharkskin or velvet)	20 - 50
D6382	Krueger Fawn, birds, chipmunk or bunny, ea.	10 - 30

1938-1941 Knickerbocker (D6390-D6420)

D6390	Western Donald	50 - 500
D6391	Mexican Mickey or Donald	60 - 600
D6393	Russian Donald	55 - 550
D6394	Major Mickey	55 - 550
D6395	Ferdinand the Bull, composition or stuffed	10 - 40
D6397	Donald's Nephews, stuffed, 2 sizes, each	5 - 35
D6400	Dwarfs, stuffed	10 - 40
D6410	Pinocchio, jointed composition or stuffed	25 - 195
D6411	Jiminy Cricket, jointed composition or stuffed	25 - 195
D6413	Figaro, jointed composition or mohair	15 - 145
D6415	Cleo the Goldfish	15 - 55
D6417	Donkey, 2 sizes	10 - 40
D6420	Dumbo	20 - 150
D6440	Crown Pinocchio, 3 composition versions	20 - 250
D6445	Ideal Pinocchio, wood jointed or "Flexy"	15 - 185
D6447	Krueger Pinocchio, wood jointed or cloth	15 - 185
D6450	Krueger Ferdinand the Bull	10 - 60
D6451	Krueger Donald w/band leader's hat	25 - 100
D6460	Steiff Bambi (3 sizes)	15 - 200
D6480	Panchito, Joe Carioca or Donald	
	(Character Novelty), each	15 - 75
D6500	Bongo or Lulubelle (1947) Gund	15 - 65
D6501	Mickey or Donald (1947) Gund	20 - 75
D6503	Pluto (1947) Gund	12 - 50
D6504	Mother Pluto and 3 pups (Gund) 1948	20 - 110
D6505	Pluto (Gund) 1949	15 - 65
D6510	Mickey or Minnie (1949) Gund (each)	25 - 125
D6512	Dumbo (1949) Gund	15 - 75
D6513	Danny the Black Lamb w/fair ribbon	15 - 75
D6514	Three Pigs (1949) Gund, each	6 - 22
D6517	Donald's Nephew's (1949) Gund (each)	10 - 25
D6525	Gus or Jaques (1950) Gund, each	10 - 45
D6526	Cinderella (1950)	25 - 100
D6529	Cinderella (1950) Story Book	10 - 45
D6530	Cinderella 2-headed topsey-turvey, 18"	20 - 85
D6550	Alice in Wonderland (1951) Movie Doll	20 - 85
D6551	Alice in Wonderland (1951) Story Book	10 - 45
D6570	Peter Pan (1952) Ideal	15 - 60
D6576	Tinkerbell (1952-59) various sizes	5 - 45
D6590	Mickey or Minnie (1952) Sun Rubber	
	w/clothes, each	5 - 20
D6625	Talking Ludwig Von Drake	50 - 200
D6650	Cinderella ″ removable heads, set	
	(1964) Horsman	20 - 80
D6651	Cinderella in ball gown (1964) Horsman	10 - 50
D6775	Small World Dolls, 12″ female characters	
	from Japan, Africa, Mexico, France, and	
	others (1963) each	5 - 30
D6800	Mary Poppins (1964) 36″ walking doll	20 - 85
D6801	Mary Poppins (1964) Horsman, 3 sets, each	15 - 50
D6835	White Rabbit promotional	10 - 50
D6850	Miniature Disney Favorites (Gund) each	1 - 7
D6862	Mickey or Minnie rag doll, each	2 - 12
D6875	Dolls by Jerri	25 - 300

Licensed manufacturers: Alexander Doll Co. (NYC) 1933-39, 1951-53 and 1959; Aurora Products Corp. (W. Hempstead, NY) 1975; George Borgfeldt & Co. (NYC) 1930-41; Cameo Doll Products Co. (Port Allegamy, PA) 1942; Character Novelty Co. (S. Norwoath, CN) 1940-47; Clopay Corp. (Cincinnati, OH) 1936-39; Cosmopolitan Doll & Toy Corp. (Jackson Hts, NY) 1955-57; Crown Toy Mfg. Co. Inc. (NYC) 1937-41; R. Dankin & Co. (SF, CA) 1972-73; Deluxe Premium Corp. (NYC) 1955-56; Dolls by Jerri (Charlotte, NC) 1982-84; Duchess Doll Corp. (LI, NY) 1951-54; Fortune Toys (NYC) 1955; Gund Manufacturing Co. (NYC) 1947-55, 1959, 1968-71; Horsman Dolls, Inc. (NYC) 1964, 1972, 1976-84; Hungerford Plastics Corp. (Rockaway, NJ) 1955-57; Ideal Novelty & Toy Co. (NYC) 1937-43, 1952-53; Knickerbocker Toy Company, Inc. (NYC) 1934-42, 1976-83; Richard Krueger (NYC) 1934-41; Plastic Molded Arts Co. (LI, NY) 1953; Ross & Ross (Oakland, CA) 1933-34; Margarete Steiff & Co. (NYC office) 1931, Imported until 1942; Sun Rubber (Barberton, OH) 1952-54; Uneeda Doll Co., Inc. (Brooklyn) 1960-62; Wallace Berrie & Co. (Van Nuys) 1984 and World Toy Mfg. Corp. (NYC) 1939-41.
Also see: FIGURES, PLUSH STUFFED TOYS.

D6835

D6500

D6862

D6625

D6850

D6875

D7801

D7808

Walt Disney's
Snow White
CUT-OUT DOLL AND DRESSES

D7805

Walt Disney's
Snow White
and the Seven Dwarfs
Paper Dolls

10¢

D7807

D7806

D7850

Walt Disney's
Pinocchio
DOLL CUT OUTS

D7810

D7875

D7862

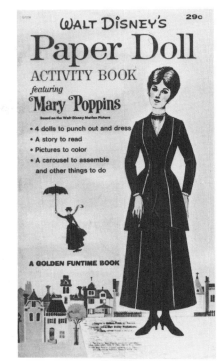

D7864

D7868

D7875

D7875

D7852

D7858

D7859

D7865

D7870

D7875

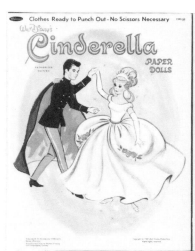

D7867

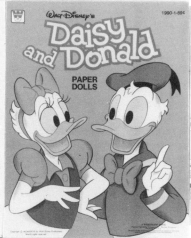

D7875

D7875

D7875

Whitman paper doll boxed sets from early 60's.

D7875

D7800 DOLLS — PAPER

Paper dolls were usually published in book form. However, boxed sets appeared as early as 1959. Saalfeld produced a Mickey and Minnie book in 1933. Whitman has been the dominant publisher ever since.

D7801	Mickey/Minnie Cut-Out Doll Book (1933)	35 - 210
D7805	Snow White Cut-Out Doll and Dresses, vertical (1938)	20 - 150
D7806	Snow White Cut-Out Doll and Dresses (1938)	20 - 150
D7807	Snow White and the Seven Dwarfs, 10¢ paper dolls (1938)	20 - 150
D7808	Snow White and the Seven Dwarfs Paper Dolls (1938)	20 - 150
D7810	Pinocchio Doll Cut Outs (1939)	20 - 130
D7850	Annette Mouseketeer Cut-Out Dolls (1958)	6 - 20
D7852	Linda Mouseketeer Cut-Out Dolls (1958)	5 - 15
D7858	Sleeping Beauty Dolls with Magic Stay-On Dresses (1959)	6 - 24
D7859	Sleeping Beauty, 6 Cut-Out Dolls (1959)	6 - 20
D7862	Pollyanna (1960)	5 - 18
D7864	Paper Doll Activity Book featuring Mary Poppins (1964)	5 - 15
D7865	Jane and Michael (Mary Poppins) 1964	5 - 15
D7867	Cinderella (1965)	5 - 15
D7868	Mary Poppins Paper Dolls (1966)	5 - 15
D7870	It's a Small World (1966)	5 - 15
D7875	Other Paper Dolls 1967-1984, each	1 - 10

D7875

D8225

D8165

D8001

D8167   D8168   D8166

19

D8204   D8209   D8200   D8208   D8192

D8195

D8198

D8030

D8170

D8214

D8220   D8265

D8215

D8000 DONALD DUCK PRODUCTS

The Florida Citrus Canners Cooperative (later Citrus World) found a unifying symbol with Donald Duck in 1941. National Oats Co. used Donald on oatmeal in 1943, followed by Nash-Underwood Mustard & Peanut Butter in 1944. By 1948 Donald Duck was endorsing over two dozen products. Mickey and the other Disney characters were used to endorse food products throughout the 30's, but food licensing became more important in the 40's. War material shortages curtailed the production of many toy items right at the time character merchandise income from animated features was becoming significant. Donald was the most popular cartoon character of the time and was featured on most products. Kay Kamen eventually formed a special division for licensing Donald Duck products. Food product merchandising was discouraged when Disney entered TV programing to avoid sponsor conflicts.

D8001	Orange juice cans, 40's	3 - 22
D8030	Other citrus drink and fruit cans, 40's	3 - 22
D8050	Citrus products, 50's and later	1 - 10
D8150	Oatmeal (1943-45)	5 - 50
D8155	Peanut butter (1944) Nash-Underwood	3 - 30
D8157	Mustard, figural jar, bank lid	5 - 50
D8160	Orange Juice container, Foremost Dairies (1946)	2 - 20
D8165	Peanut butter (1947) Cinderella Foods	3 - 22
D8166	Salad dressing	3 - 22
D8167	Mayonnaise	3 - 22
D8168	Sandwich spread	3 - 22
D8170	Rice, packaged	4 - 40
D8190	Macaroni or spaghetti	4 - 40
D8192	Apple juice, apple butter, or applesauce	3 - 35
D8195	Coffee	3 - 35
D8196	Peas or canned field peas, Chowder	3 - 22
D8198	Mustard	3 - 22
D8199	Pimentos	3 - 30
D8200	Catsup, cocktail sauce or chili sauce	3 - 35
D8204	Tomato juice, various sizes	3 - 30
D8208	Whole tomatoes, canned	3 - 30
D8209	Tomato puree	3 - 30
D8210	Corn, canned	3 - 30

D8190

D8275

D8050

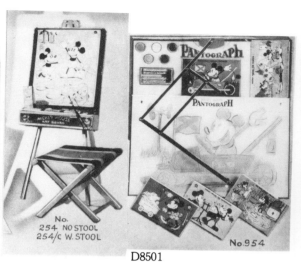

D8501

D8290

D9020

D9010

Interesting drawing set from late 70's. Value 1 - 5.

D8600

D9030

D9040

E1530

D8610

E1500

D8211	Pumpkin, canned	3 - 30
D8214	Corn syrup (Atlantic)	3 - 30
D8215	Chocolate flavor syrup (Atlantic)	3 - 30
D8220	Corn syrup products (American)	3 - 30
D8225	Bread, various bakeries	4 - 40
D8260	Popcorn	5 - 20
D8265	Cola or other soft drinks	4 - 16
D8266	Soft drink six bottle carton	40 - 80
D8267	Bottle caps, each	.25 - 2
D8268	Promotional glass, each	2 - 10
D8275	Frozen confection bags	1 - 9
D8290	Donald Duck products, Labels only	1 - 15

E1515

D8505

Licensed manufacturers: Atlantic Syrup Refining Corp. (Philadelphia) 1949-54, corn syrup products; American Syrup & Sorghum Co. (St. Louis) 1949-50, corn syrup products; Bowman Apple Products Co., Inc. (Mt. Jackson, VA) 1948-50, apple juice, applesauce and apple butter; Cinderella Foods — see Stevens Industries; Citrus World, Inc. (Lake Wales, FL) 1977-84, fruit juices, fruit salads, plus frozen, canned, and fresh fruit; Delmonico Foods, Inc. (Louisville, KY) 1948-50, macaroni and spaghetti products; J.H.Erbrich Products Co. (Indianapolis, IN) 1949-50, mustard products; Florida Citrus Canners Cooperative (Lake Wales, FL) 1941-76 — see Citrus World Inc.; Foremost Dairies (Jacksonville, FL) 1946-47, orange juice; Fruit Products Corp. (NYC) wrappers for frozen confections; General Beverages, Inc. (Chattanooga, TN) 1952-55, cola and soft drinks; Goyer Company (Greenvile, MS) 1948-50, coffee; Harnell Brothers Canning Co. (Eastman, GA) 1948-50, canned field peas, chowder, peas and pimentos; Kay Kamen Ltd. (NYC) 1949-50, Donald Duck Bread campaign; Naas Corp. (Portland, IN) 1948-53, canned and bottled tomato products, added canned corn and pumpkin in 1953; Nash-Underwood, Inc. (1944-47), mustard and peanut butter; National Oats Co. (Cedar Rapids, IA) 1943-45, oatmeal; Popcorn Sales, Inc. (Carnoivon, IA) 1949-50, popcorn; Producers Rice Mill, Inc. (Stuttgart, AR) 1947-60, packaged rice; Southeastern Foods, Inc. (Andalusia, AL) 1947-53, salad dressing, mayonnaise, and sandwich spread; Stevens Industries, Inc. a.k.a. Cinderella Foods (Dawson, GA) 1948-50, peanut butter; and World Citrus West, Inc. (Fullerton, CA) 1981-84, Donald Duck orange juice, additional licensee.

D8500 DRAWING SETS & MATERIALS

A drawing set differs from a crayon, coloring, or paint set. Drawing sets, by various means, facilitate the actual drawing or creating of the Disney character. The set usually contains pictures to be reproduced in some manner along with a "desk", light table, or a drawing device.

D8501	Marx Pantograph #954	25 - 110
D8505	Dixon Mystery Art Set #2900	22 - 85
D8600	Mousekartooner (Mattel)	4 - 15
D8610	Toon-A-Vision designer (1968)	2 - 15
D8625	Light Up Drawing Desk (Lakeside)	3 - 18

E1510

Licensed manufacturers — American Creative Toys, Inc. (NYC) 1975; AMSCO Industries (Hatboro, PA) 1968, 72 Toon-A-Vision; Joseph Dixon Crucible Co. (Jersey City, NJ) 1931-42; Lakeside Industries, Inc. division of Leisure Dynamics (Minneapolis, MN) 1962-82; Marx Brothers Co. (Boston) 1934-41; and Mattel, Inc. (LA) 1955.

D9000 DRUMS

One way kids can always get attention is by beating a drum. Mickey has provided a wide variety of metal and conventional drums. Ohio Art was the major producer of metal versions. Noble & Cooley Co. has traditionally provided other types.

D9010	Metal drums 7", each	10 - 70
D9020	Metal drums 12", each	15 - 100
D9030	Illustrated drum head or Band Drum	30 - 200
D9040	Drum set	50 - 800

E1540 E1541 D9010

Licensed manufacturers — Noble and Cooley Co. (Granville, MA) 1935-39, 1969-83 and Ohio Art Co. (Bryan, OH) 1933-42, 1944-45, 1982.

E1500 EASTER EGG DYE & TRANSFER SETS

Paas Dye Company originated this product category in 1936 and continued until 1955. They also made tattoos and albums for year round use. Not until the recent Egg Art creation has there been a superior product.

E1500	Transfer-O's for Easter eggs (30's)	5 - 25
E1510	Paas pure food Easter egg colors (1947)	8 - 27
E1515	Paas complete Easter egg decorating kit	15 - 45
E1530	Easter egg colors w/figural bottles (Chemtoy)	3 - 15
E1540	Egg Art — Mickey (Sun Hill)	1 - 3
E1541	Egg Art — Bambi (Sun Hill)	1 - 3

Licensed manufacturers — Chemtoy Corp. (Chicago) 1970-81; Paas Dye

E5000

E5000

Walt Disney World
EPCOT
CENTER

E6009

E5000   E6079

E6080

E6112 E6111

E6110 E6111 E6112

E6090

E6082

E6001

E6008

E6800

E6020   E6021

E6400

24

Co. (Newark, NJ) 1936-55 and Sun Hill Industries, Inc. (Stanford, CT) 1982-84.

E6005   E6006

E5000 EMPLOYEE PUBLICATIONS

Disney is a big organization. Each of the major divisions has a "house organ" publication for its employees. The employees of Disneyland receive *The Disneyland Line*. A similar publication in Florida is the Walt Disney World *Eyes and Ears*. Studio employees receive the *Disney Newsreel*. Employees in all divisions for a time received *The Disney Times*, in a newspaper format. Theme park cast members also received a quarterly magazine that had several names over the years. Special events usually prompt more spectacular versions of the regular house organs. There are also numerous special employee relations publications detailing a company policy. There have been some interesting historical booklets as well. It's interesting to collect samples of this material; however, they have little value.

E6000 EPCOT CENTER

Walt Disney's grandest dream, an Experimental Prototype Community Of Tomorrow, remains largely unfulfilled. A model of his concept is now called a city of the future when viewed from the PeopleMover attraction at Walt Disney World. Walt envisioned a planned city where new innovations in transportation, services, engineering, construction, and quality of life could be put into practice. Unfortunately, his vision for realizing his dream died with him. The city of Lake Buena Vista incorporates some of his ideas, but the master plan is missing.

Instead there is EPCOT Center, a showcase for new ideas incorporated into a permanent World's Fair type setting. EPCOT Center is educational. Journey into Imagination stands out with many new entertainment concepts. The Land treats its subjects well. Universe of Energy has some great moments. The rest, while impressive, is a background of history and commercialism that doesn't generate much collectible merchandise. World Showcase would become an overnight success for collectors if Disney licensed merchandise from the various countries were on sale, but the practice is prohibited as of this writing.

E6018

E6001	Pre-opening brochure	5 - 20
E6005	Pre-opening souvenir book w/ads	2 - 7
E6006	First year souvenir book w/o ads	2 - 7

(EPCOT Center combined with Walt Disney World Souvenir book w/o ads after the opening year)

E6007	Opening day employee publication	1 - 4
E6008	EPCOT Center, hardback	5 - 15
E6009	Newspaper inserts, each	2 - 10
E6010	Opening day VIP book	5 - 15
E6012	Opening day ticket (Oct. 1, 1982)	3 - 10
E6013	Souvenir ticket paperweight	25 - 35
E6014	same as E6013, but embedded in lucite	25 - 50
E6018	Set of 2 collector's plates (Ltd. to 7500)	75 - 100
E6020	Giveaway guide booklet w/wheel	2 - 6
E6021	Giveaway guide booklet 2nd and 3rd versions	1 - 2
E6030	Opening day foil sticker	1 - 3
E6050	Pre-opening coin	5 - 15
E6051	Employee coin in folder	5 - 15
E6052	Souvenir coin	1 - 4
E6060	Postcards, set of 14 pre-opening, drawings	20 - 30
E6061	Postcards, post opening photo cards, each	.10 - .50
E6079	Pinback buttons, construction, set of 3	10 - 25
E6080	Pinback buttons, opening day, employee, each	10 - 25
E6082	Pinback buttons, Future World logos, 1-1/2", each	3 - 5
E6090	Pinback buttons, Future World logos, 2-1/2", each	4 - 6
E6110	Pinback button, Spaceship Earth, 2"	1 - 5
E6111	Pinback button, Future World, 3"	.50 - 3
E6112	Pinback button, World Showcase, 3"	.50 - 3
E6113	Pinback button, logo, 2 color varieties, each	.50 - 3
E6175	Sweater pins, plastic, each	.50 - 3
E6225	Cloisonne pins, each	.50 - 3
E6299	World of Motion tab, each	.25 - 1
E6300	Patches, each	1 - 4
E6400	License plate or holder, each	1 - 3
E6425	Dreamfinder and Figment figure, bronze	100 - 250
E6426	Same as E6425 with pen holder	100 - 250
E6450	Key chains, each	.50 - 2
E6480	Magnets, each	.50 - 1

E6574

E6007

E6495

E6010

25

F1001

F1005

F1020

F1008

F1010

F1030

F1041

F1050

F1040

F1070

F0500

F1090

F1085

F1089

F1118

F1088

F1092

26

E6495	Stationery set with pen	1 - 5
E6500	Figment, stuffed, various sizes	2 - 18
E6550	Figment hat	4 - 10
E6574	Coloring book	1 - 2
E6575	Figment souvenirs, miscellaneous	.50 - 10
E6700	EPCOT Center apparel	5 - 100
E6800	Paper park supplies, with logos	.25 - 5
E6860	Watches, children	3 - 25
E6861	Watches, collectors	50 - 250

F0500 FABRIC

Yardgoods with Disney characters have been produced in cotton, linen, rayon, cretonne, chintz, marquisette, knits, silk, vinyl, rayon crepe and other synthetic fibers. Nashua Manufacturing built a line around Snow White in 1938 and Interchemical Corporation used characters to promote "fabric finishes" in 1947. Fabrics were most popular in the earlier years when more mothers found time to sew blankets, drapes, pajamas, and playwear. Fabric made before 1945 is seldom found, but later designs pop up and sell for about the going price of yardgoods.

Licensed manufacturers — Bates Fabrics, Inc. (NYC) 1955-56, 1979-83; Arthur Beir & Company, Inc. (NYC); Cohn-Hall-Marx (NYC) 1938-41; Colcombet-Werk, Inc. (NYC) 1937-39; Cone Export & Commission Co. (NYC) 1938-40; Continella Industries Corp. (NYC) 1970-71; Flexington Corp. (NYC) 1952-53; G. Hand E. Freyberg, Inc. (NYC) 1933-34; Henry Glass & Co., Inc. (NYC) 1952-53; Interchemical Corp. (?) 1947-48 (fabric finishes); Nashua Mfg. Co. (Sold linens through ads depicting Snow White and the Seven Dwarfs) 1938-39; Louis Nessel & Co., Inc. (NYC) 1938-39; Seneca Textile Corp. (NYC) 1933-34; Stehli & Co., Inc. (NYC) 1939-40; Travis Fabrics, Inc. (NYC) 1955-56; and Valentine Textile Corp. (NYC) 1937-38.

F1000 FAN CARDS

A fan card is a free promotional illustration or photo that is sent to fans who send fan letters or otherwise request a photo. It was a popular pastime to do so in the 30's and continues to date. In recent years the size has been reduced. Cards were produced for all animated features and most live action films. The animated character cards are the most prized and collected.

F1001	Mickey and Butch (Newspaper offer)	10 - 80
F1005	Mickey-Sincerely Yours	10 - 60
F1008	Mickey and Minnie	10 - 60
F1010	Mickey and Pluto	10 - 50
F1020	Mickey, Pluto and 3 Pigs	10 - 50
F1030	Donald	8 - 45
F1040	Snow White and the Seven Dwarfs	5 - 22
F1041	Dopey	5 - 22
F1048	Snow White and the Seven Dwarfs premium	2 - 12
F1050	Pinocchio and Jiminy Cricket	5 - 22
F1055	Pinocchio premium	2 - 12
F1070	Bambi	4 - 20
F1085	Song of the South	5 - 25
F1088	Fun and Fancy Free	5 - 25
F1089	Melody Time	5 - 25
F1090	So Dear to My Heart	4 - 20
F1092	The Adventures of Ichabod and Mr. Toad	5 - 25
F1095	Cinderella	5 - 25
F1097	Alice In Wonderland	5 - 25
F1098	Peter Pan	2 - 14
F1099	Walt Disney	5 - 25
F1100	Mickey's 25th Birthday	1 - 3
F1105	Lady and the Tramp	2 - 8
F1106	Lady and the Tramp (reissue)	1 - 5
F1115	Sleeping Beauty	2 - 8
F1118	Shaggy Dog	1 - 4
F1125	101 Dalmatians	2 - 8
F1136	The Sword in the Stone	2 - 8
F1138	Donald engineer	1 - 2
F1139	Mickey and Pluto at the fireplace	2 - 8
F1148	Mary Poppins	1 - 5
F1155	The Jungle Book	2 - 8
F1160	The Love Bug	1 - 5
F1162	Walt Disney and main characters	1 - 7
F1165	Winnie the Pooh	1 - 4
F1170	The Aristocats	1 - 4
F1173	Mickey (costumed) at Walt Disney World	1 - 4
F1175	Bedknobs and Broomsticks	1 - 4

F1095

F1105

F1097

F1098

F1099

F1180

F1139

F1138

F1203

F1190

F1162

F1100

F1200

F1170

F1106

F1178

F1215

F1201

F1165

F1173

F1902

F2022

F1500

F2040

F2041

F2005

F2006

F1903

SURPRISE!

F1919

F1918

F1922

F1921

F1925

F1923

F1928

F1920

F1178	Robin Hood	1 - 6
F1180	50 Happy Years	2 - 8
F1185	New Mickey Mouse Club	1 - 3
F1188	The Rescuers	1 - 4
F1190	Pete's Dragon	1 - 4
F1192	Mousekedays at Disneyland	1 - 3
F1200	Mickey's 50th portrait (EPCOT Center)	1 - 2
F1201	Mickey's 50	1 - 5
F1203	Snow White (reissue)	1 - 3
F1205	The Fox and the Hound	1 - 3
F1208	TRON	1 - 3
F1210	Mickey's Christmas Carol	1 - 3
F1215	Splash	1 - 3

F1500 FANS

Paperboard advertising hand fans were made during the Silly Symphony era (probably by a calendar licensee), and one was made for America On Parade. H. P. Incorporated (Ramonda, CA) made an electric ceiling fan in 1984. The 30's fans are valued at 15 -50.

F1900 50TH BIRTHDAY — DONALD DUCK

"The Wise Little Hen" introduced Donald Duck in 1934. A year long birthday party was held at Disney theme parks in 1984 to celebrate the 50 year old event. Merchandise and publicity wasn't as extensive as it was for Mickey's 50th, but some nice items resulted.

F1901	Collector's plate, large, Grolier	25 - 30
F1902	Collector's plate, large, theme park	20 - 35
F1903	Collector's plates, small, set of 3	20 - 50
F1906	T-shirt	2 - 10
F1908	Watches, regular issue	10 - 25
F1911	Watches, Limited edition	35 - 95
F1913	Watch, digital premium/Donald Duck orange juice	5 - 12
F1918	Coloring book	1 - 4
F1919	Birthday cake promotion piece	1 - 2
F1920	Pinback button, blue, sold with cake	2 - 10
F1921	Pinback button, blue with Chip 'n Dale and yellow rim	3 - 15
F1922	Same as F1921, but with HP Books	3 -18
F1923	Same as F1921, but Ice Show with black line and blue ribbon	4 - 20
F1925	Unauthorized button	2 - 10
F1928	City of Glendale Rose Parade lapel pin	5 - 20
F1930	Disney Channel lapel pin	20 - 25
F1980	Paper cups & plates, each	1 - 2

F2000 50TH BIRTHDAY — MICKEY MOUSE

Fifty years after Mickey's debut November 18, 1928 at New York's Colony Theater, one of the world's largest birthday parties was held. The focal point was Disneyland, but the event was marked worldwide in newspapers, magazines, theaters, a TV special and at Walt Disney World. There was a tremendous buildup to the event with a special cross-continent train, publicity, films and, of course, merchandise. In an unusual departure from proven promotion and merchandise techniques, five different logos were used for the event: 1) silhouette of Mickey against a wrapped package; 2) Mickey lighting candles on a birthday cake, used on Schmid and other merchandise; 3) a cake with Mickey's face surrounded by characters; 4) a big 50 with Mickeys and 5) Mickey in a party hat with lettering — "Happy Birthday Mickey — 50 years."

F2001	Book, Mickey Mouse Fifty Happy Years (hard or soft)	2 - 12
F2003	Press kit, (Big 50) cover, booklet, photos and releases	3 - 25
F2004	Disney News or Vacationland	1 - 2
F2005	Coloring book	1 - 5
F2006	Comic books with package logo, each	1 - 3
F2008	May Co. comic contest entry folder and card	2 - 8
F2010	Magazines with 50th birthday covers	1 - 5
F2011	Employee publications, each	1 - 5
F2012	Corporate annual report	2 - 8
F2015	Mickey's Birthday Storyfest	2 - 10

F2003

F2050

F2012

F2004

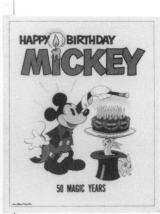

50 MAGIC YEARS

F2008

F2035

F2075

F2030

F2023

F2032

F2071

F2065

F2555

F2556

F2031

F2024

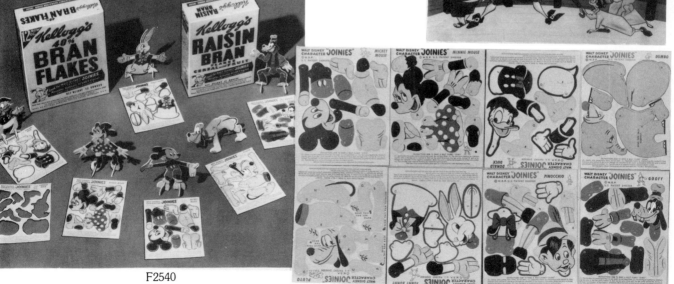

F2540

F2540

F2016	Disneyland or Walt Disney World guide books	1 - 5
F2018	Vinyl ribbon for employee name tag	2 - 12
F2019	Tie	3 - 12
F2020	T-shirt	3 - 12
F2021	Pajamas or other apparel	4 - 15
F2022	Decal (Big 50)	1 - 3
F2023	Promotional sticker (party hat)	1 - 4
F2024	Stickers, theater ushers, set of 6	10 - 40
F2025	Wristwatch Quartz registered number edition, boxed	50 - 100
F2026	Wristwatch — Bradley Time	10 - 50
F2029	Clock	10 - 40
F2030	Pinback button, 1" promotional	10 - 35
F2031	Pinback button, 3" cake logo, either theme park	2 - 10
F2032	Pinback button, "Mickey and I are 50 this year"	25 - 100
F2033	Pinback, VIP givaway	2 - 15
F2035	Movie, limited edition, numbered	25 - 75
F2040	Collector's plate, Mickey lighting candles (10,000) Schmid	15 - 50
F2041	Collector's plate, birthday cake with characters (3,000)	20 - 60
F2050	Doll (Remco)	5 - 25
F2051	Doll with Happy Birthday shirt (California Stuffed Toys)	5 - 25
F2052	Plush Mickey's with package logo tag	4 - 20
F2055	Music box (Schmid)	10 - 50
F2056	Christmas tree ornament	5 - 20
F2058	Waste basket	3 - 18
F2059	Cookie jar	10 - 40
F2060	Glass tumblers, set of six, Pepsi promotion	6 - 15
F2062	Mug, plastic, birthday cake logo	2 - 10
F2063	Dinnerware, 3 piece sets, Melamine, each	4 - 12
F2065	Puzzles, 5 different, each	1 - 6
F2070	School supplies, tablets, folders and notebooks, each	1 - 5
F2071	Coloring contest drawing	1 - 4
F2075	Magnet, package logo	2 - 10
F2076	Yo-yo	2 - 10
F2079	Needlepoint kit	3 - 15
F2090	Pennant, (Big 50) Disneyland	2 - 10
F2095	Poster, (Big 50) Disneyland party	3 - 15
F2096	Program, Disneyland party	2 - 10
F2098	Paper or foam cups, each	1 - 4
F2100	Paper plates, each	1 - 5
F2101	Sandwich bag, hot dog or frozen banana wrapper	1 - 4
F2102	Matches, each	.25 - .50
F2105	Boyer print of painting presented to Walt Disney's widow (limited to 1800)	50 - 500
F2110	Lithographs of Mickey's 25th and 50th birthday oil portraits by John Hench. In gold stamped commemorative portfolio. Sold for $50 to employees whose names were drawn for the right to purchase. Limited to 750.	100 - 700

F2500 FIGURES — CARDBOARD

F2510	Movie studio (Standard Toykraft)	25 - 75
F2520	Hingees (King, Larson & McMahon) Came individual envelope or in set with other comic characters Individual	4 - 18
	Set 15 - 60	
F2530	Slotties (CCA) set of 6	10 - 40
F2540	Joinies (CCA) Kellogg Raisin Bran premiums. Original set of 8, plus vocational set of ? each	3 - 8
F2555	Alice in Wonderland, stand-up figures (Whitman) set of 15, #5613	5 - 25
F2556	Peter Pan playtime statuettes (Whitman) set of 11, #5616	5 - 25
F2600	Mickey Mouse Peg Pals (Colorforms) 1978	1 - 4

Licensed manufacturers — Childhood Interests, Inc. (Roselle Pk., NJ) 1955-57; Colorforms (Norwood, NJ) 1977; Container Corporation of America (Chicago) 1944-46, 1948-50; W.H.Greene Co. (Chicago) 1943-45; King Larson & McMahon (Chicago) 1944-46; Standard Toykraft Products, Inc. (Brooklyn, NY) 1939-41; and Whitman Publishing Co. (Racine, WI) 1952-54 for stand-up figures.

Also see — BOOKS — CUT OR PUNCH OUT and DOLLS — PAPER

F2520

F2510

MICKEY MOUSE PEG PALS

F2600

F2530

ENESCO IMPORTS, INC.

A Gorgeous Array of Colorful "Snow White Ceramics." Items retail $1.00 to $5.00.

F3400

F3340

F3540

F3542

0553-9020

0553-9019

0553-9022

0553-9021

0553-9034

0553-9035

0553-9036

F3547

F3545

Pencil Pot Sharpener WDE-108

Planter or Kiddies' Overnighter WDE-106 3½" x 3" x 5"

WDE-110 Savings Bank 6½" high

F3400

WDE 114

5½" high Ornaments air activated Semi-porcelain

F6030

F6035

F6031

F6033

F6034

F6109

F6110

F6080

F6064

F6063

F6071

F6068

F6072

F6070

F6069

F6088   F6120   F6013

F6095   F6122   F6048

F6010   F6011   F6087   F6012

F6032

F6190

F6021   F6027   F6026   F6025   F6024   F6020

F6009

F6086

F6008

F6095

F6048

F6007

F6085

F6040

F6090

F6091

F6041

F6153

F6178

F6179

F6183

F6162

F6060

F6053

F6062

F6177

F6103

F6175

F6147

F6148

F6061

F6054

F6105

F6135

F6136

F6137

F6104

F6049

F6102

F6138

F6145

F6144

F6100

F6006

F6101

F6160

F6143

F6050

F6096

F6047

F6094

F6121

F6157

F6159

F6158

F6156

F6052

F6185

F6001

F6275

F6150

F6092

F3000 FIGURES — CELLULOID

Celluloid was an early plastic-like substance. Two types of figures are produced from this material — miniature solid pieces and the more recognized thin, hollow figures. They were produced from the early 30's to the early 50's — mainly in Japan. The major importer was Borgfeldt. Celluloid wind-up toys were perhaps more common than static figures and celluloid figures were used on some tin wind-up and mechanical toys of the 40's and 50's.

F3011	Mickey 5", movable arms	50 - 175
F3012	Minnie 5", movable arms	50 - 175
F3015	Donald and Mickey in boat	50 - 200
F3025	Donald 3", long bill, movable arms and legs	15 - 50
F3026	Donald 5", long bill, movable arms and legs	20 - 80
F3031	Mickey, pie-cut eyes, no moving parts, various sizes	20 - 150
F3034	Donald, long bill, no moving parts, various sizes	20 - 150
F3048	Cleo the Goldfish	10 - 30
F3050	Mickey, regular eyes	10 - 50
F3060	Donald, regular eyes, short bill	10 - 50

Also see — NODDERS and WINDUP TOYS

F3300 FIGURES — CERAMIC

Major ceramic makers such as American Pottery, Brayton's Laguna Pottery, Leeds China Company, Evan K Shaw, National Porcelain Company, Hagen-Renaker and Vernon Kilns are listed in their own classifications. Bisque figures are also listed separately. What remains is largely an unidentified group of foreign manufacturers and importers. Some from the early 30's and others who have supplied ceramic figures to the Disney theme parks since 1955. The 30's pieces were made mainly in Japan and Germany and imported by Borgfeldt. A Tinker Bell piece from the 50's has a foil sticker that reads "Ucago Ceramics — Japan." Another Mickey piece has the letters "UCGC — Japan." Pieces available in the parks in the 70's are simply marked with a copyright notice and the word "Japan." Some pieces from the 60's and 70's are credited to Enesco Imports, Inc. An Enesco *Baloo* figurine is copyright 1965. During the 70's ceramic figure designs for popular characters changed every 2 or 3 years. Catalog stock numbers are shown for 70's and 80's figures, when available. The 0553 item code prefix has been deleted. These numbers appeared in catalogs and on the original price tag only. Sizes and numbers for identical looking pieces did change. The author is indebted to Stan Pawlowski for the information and photos provided for the various California ceramic manufacturers.

F3305	Mickey with teeth, various sizes	35 - 150
F3310	Mickey band, gold or colored instruments, 1 1/4", each	10 - 70
F3320	Mickey figures, Germany	10 - 300
F3330	Mickey figures, Japan, up to 7"	10 - 250
F3340	Ucago figures, each	4 - 60
F3400	Enesco figures, each	2 - 40
F3500	Mickey (9017), Minnie (9018), or Pluto (0333), each	2 - 8
F3503	Mickey (0327) or Minnie (0328), pie-cut eyes, each	2 - 8
F3506	Donald (0329), Daisy (9050), or nephews (9051), each	2 - 8
F3511	Uncle Scrooge (9049)	1 - 6
F3515	Alice (9016), White Rabbit (9001) or Cheshire Cat (9023), each	2 - 8
F3518	Mad Hatter (9000) or March Hare (9003), each	2 - 10
F3525	Snow White, lifting dress (0332)	2 - 10
F3526	Seven Dwarfs, standing (9008-9014), each	1 - 7
F3540	Lady (9019) or Tramp (9020), each	2 - 8
F3542	Trusty (9021) or Jock (9022), each	1 - 5
F3545	Pongo (9034) or Perdita (9035), each	2 - 10
F3547	Dalmatian Pups, six different (9036), each	1 - 3
F3555	Mary Poppins (0017)	2 - 7
F3556	Tinker Bell (0331), Bambi (0018) or Dumbo (9002), each	1 - 6
F3560	Pinocchio (9015) or Jiminy Cricket (9007), each	1 - 6
F3562	Jaq (9004) or Gus (9006), each	1 - 6
F3564	Brer Fox, Brer Rabbit or Brer Bear, set	10 - 40
F3570	Cinderella (9467) or Prince, kneeling (9468), each	2 - 10
F3572	Gus (9469) or Jaq (9470), each	1 - 6
F3575	Snow White, standing (9459) 5-1/2"	1 - 8
F3576	Seven Dwarfs, standing, sitting and reclining (9460-9466), each	1 - 4

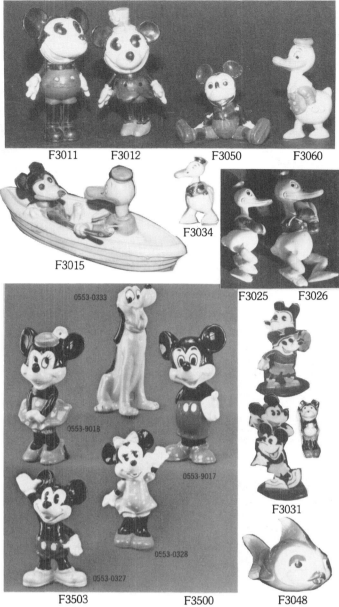

F3011   F3012   F3050   F3060

F3034

F3015

F3025   F3026

F3031

F3048

0553-0333

0553-9018

0553-9017

0553-0328

0553-0327

F3503   F3500

0553-0329

0553-9050

0553-9049

0553-9051

F3511   F3506

41

F3518

F3555

0553-9000
0553-9003
0553-9016
0553-9005
0553-9023

0553-0017
0553-9007
0553-9015
0553-0331
0553-0018
0553-9002
0553-9006
0553-9004

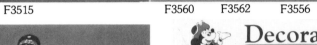

F4710

F3515

F3560   F3562   F3556

0553-9013
0553-9009
0553-9010
0553-0332
0553-9012
0553-9014
0553-9011
0553-9008

F3526   F3525

Decorative Gifts

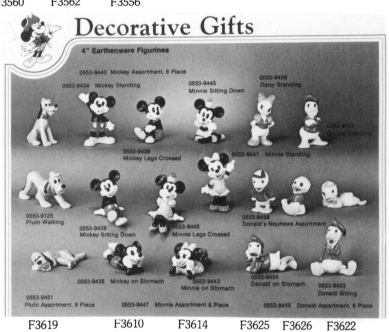

4" Earthenware Figurines

0553-9440 Mickey Assortment, 6 Piece

0553-9434 Mickey Standing
0553-9445 Minnie Sitting Down
0553-9458 Daisy Standing

0553-9438 Mickey Legs Crossed
0553-9441 Minnie Standing
0553-9452 Donald Standing

0553-9125 Pluto Walking
0553-9439 Mickey Sitting Down
0553-9446 Minnie Legs Crossed
0553-9456 Donald's Nephews Assortment

0553-9436 Mickey on Stomach
0553-9443 Minnie on Stomach
0553-9454 Donald on Stomach
0553-9453 Donald Sitting

0553-9451 Pluto Assortment, 6 Piece
0553-9447 Minnie Assortment 6 Piece
0553-9455 Donald Assortment, 6 Piece

F3619   F3610   F3614   F3625   F3626   F3622

F3564

MERRY CHRISTMAS FROM DISNEY

Royal Orleans Bisque and Ceramic figures. Value 2 - 10.

2″ Earthenware figurines

F3580	Mickey, standing (9490), resting (9491) or sitting (9492), each	1 - 4
F3583	Minnie, standing (9493), sitting (9494) or bowing (9495), each	1 - 4
F3586	Pluto, sitting (9496) or laying down (9497), each	1 - 4
F3588	Donald, standing with left arm raised (9498)	1 - 4

3″ Earthenware figurines, Mickey's band (12)

F3590	Mickey, band leader (9550), with tuba (9551) or with trumpet (9552), each	1 - 5
F3593	Minnie, with drums (9553), cymbals (9554) or sax (9555), each	1 - 5
F3596	Goofy, with bass (9556) or bass drum (9557), each	1 - 5
F3598	Donald with trumpet (9558) or guitar (9559), each	1 - 5
F3600	Daisy, with sax (9560) or flute (9561), each	1 - 5

4″ Earthenware figurines

F3610	Mickey, pie-cut eyes, standing (9434), legs crossed (9438) sitting down, dangling legs (9439) or on stomach (9436), each	2 - 8
F3614	Minnie, pie-cut eyes, standing (9441), sitting, legs to one side (9445), legs crossed (9446) or on stomach (9443)	2 - 6
F3619	Pluto, sitting (?), walking (9125) or laying down (?), each	2 - 6
F3622	Donald, standing (9452), sitting (9453) or on stomach (9454), each	2 - 6
F3625	Daisy, standing (9456)	2 - 6
F3626	Nephews, standing, sitting or on stomach, set	5 - 15

Licensed manufacturers — Allied Associate (NYC) 1941-42; Enesco Imports, Inc. (Chicago) 1965-71; Leisuramics, Inc. (Haverhill, MA) Ceramic paint yourself figures, 1972-79; and McMaster Pottery Ltd. (Canadian) 1949-50, produced figures from molds of Shaw, Leeds, and perhaps other designers.

F4700 FIGURES — COMPOSITION

Some of the very first Mickey Mouse figures were made of wood composition — basically a material of sawdust mixed with paste — similar to papier-mache. Composition figures were molded, dried and painted. If the paint was damaged, moisture could get to the composition material and cause the figure to decompose. Therefore, surviving specimens are usually in fairly good condition. Composition was widely used for doll heads, torsos, and complete figures.

F4705	Barefoot Mickey, 2-1/2″	15 - 100
F4710	Mickey with lollypop hands	50 - 800
F4715	Dixon pencil holder	5 - 70
F4716	Dixon pencil and eraser holder	5 - 70
F4720	Mickey from Lionel Circus Train set	8 - 80
F4724	Knickerbocker Mickey without a costume	50 - 250
F4725	Knickerbocker Donald without a costume	25 - 200
F4735	Seven Dwarfs, each	10 - 35

Knickerbocker Ferdinand, Pinocchio, Jiminy Cricket, Figaro, plus costumed versions of Donald and Mickey see D6335 thru D6420

Crown and Ideal Pinocchios see D6440 and D6445
Also see WIND-UP TOYS

F4850 FIGURES — DELL

Dell Distributing, Inc. (NYC) division of Dell Publishing marketed a line of hollow rubber figures circa 1959-62. They are interesting in their mold complexity and detail of some designs.

F4851	Mickey squeeze toy	2 - 10
F4852	Donald squeeze toy	2 - 10
F4853	Dumbo squeeze toy	2 - 10
F4854	Shaggy Dog squeeze toy	2 - 10
F4855	Ludwig Von Drake squeeze toy	3 - 15
F4860	Sleeping Beauty squeeze toy	4 - 20
F4861	Uncle Scrooge and nephews bank	3 - 18
F4863	Mickey and Donald soap dish	3 - 15

F4900 FIGURES — VENDING MACHINE INJECTED MOLDED

Around the time Disneyland was opening, a vending machine was developed to produce figures on the spot. Today, these are commonplace in zoos, museums and other tourist attractions.

Decorative Gifts

F3575   F3576

F3570   F3572

Decorative Gifts

F3588   F3580   F3583   F3586

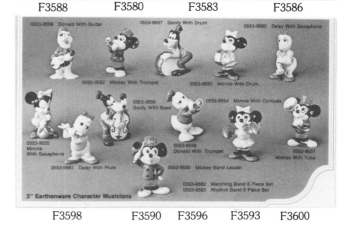

F3598   F3590   F3596   F3593   F3600

F4851   F4855   F4854   F4853

F4861   F4860   F4863

F4900

F5000

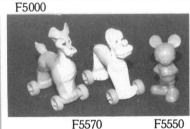

F5570   F5550

F5690

F5570

F5583

F6192   F6193   F6261

Some people remember these machines being located at Disneyland, others at non-park locations. There are 6 different figures — Mickey, Donald, Pluto, Goofy, Pinocchio, and Jiminy Cricket. They are valued at 1 - 5 each.

F5000 FIGURES — PEWTER

Calhoun's Collector's Society (St. Paul, MN) marketed a set of Hall of Presidents pewter figures in 1975-76. Schmid Brothers, Inc. (Boston) cast the first pewter Disney figures in 1976. The line has been fairly extensive, but sales sluggish. Values 8 - 20 each, some higher. Hudson is an 80's brand name. Value 3-15 each.

F5500 FIGURES — PLASTIC

Plastic figures date from the 40's. Louis Marx & Co. started producing a line of plastic figures in 1953. Many varieties were produced over the next 25 years — painted and unpainted. Original unpainted Marx figures reappeared in the mid-60's as Disney Fun Pals. Smaller versions of the same designs were sold as Disneykins (See D4000). New figures were created for Marx Playsets (See P3850). The last series (1971-72) consisted of 10 unpainted 5"-6" figures. Durham, Multiple Products, Sutton and other toy makers have produced a wide variety of plastic figures for individual sale and as part of other toy products.

F5550	Hard plastic, 2-3/4", each	1 - 5
F5570	Hard plastic on wheels, each	2 - 6
F5600	Marx unpainted, 1-1/4" to 2-3/4", Mickey, Minnie, Morty, Ferdie, Donald, Daisy, Huey, Louie, Dewey, Pluto, Snow White, Seven Dwarfs, Pinocchio, Jiminy Cricket, Geppetto, Figaro, Blue Fairy, Dumbo, Timothy, Ringmaster, Fireman Clown, Clown, Alice, Queen of Hearts, White Rabbit, Mad Hatter, March Hare, Peter Pan, Captain Hook, Smee and Tinker Bell, each	1 - 5
	Disney Fun Pals, same as F5600, painted, each	1 - 5
	Additional Fun Pals — Goofy, Pecos Bill, Panchito and others, each	1 - 5
F5670	Big Bad Wolf and Three Pigs, painted, each	2 - 6
F5675	Robin Hood Marx figures, each	1 - 5
F5685	Davy Crockett Marx figures, each	2 - 10
F5690	Marx Snap-eeze moveable figures of Mickey, Donald, Pluto, Dalmatian, Mad Hatter, March Hare, Babes in Toyland Soldier, Captain Hook, Panchito, Practical Pig, Figaro, Brer Bear, Brer Fox, Dopey and Ludwig Von Drake, each	2 - 7
F5725	Zorro and horse	3 - 15
F5730	Donald Duck's Express and figures (1968)	2 - 12
F5731	Mowgli's Hut-Mobile and figures (1968)	2 - 12
F5732	Mickey Mouse's Tin Lizzie and figures (1968)	2 - 12
F5733	Donald Duck's Whirlybird and figures (1968)	2 - 12
F5734	Mickey Mouse's Hot Rod and figures (1968)	2 - 12
F5570	Marx 5" - 7" figures — Mickey, Minnie, Donald, Goofy, Pluto, Snow White, Dopey, Pinocchio, Jiminy Cricket, Bambi, Peter Pan, and Tinker Bell (1971-72), each	1 - 3
F5583	Same as F5570, but painted — eyes only total figure	1 - 3

Licensed manufacturers — Aviva Enterprises (San Francisco) 1970-71; Durham Industries (NYC) 1972-83; Louis Marx & Co., Inc. (NYC) figures, 1953-72; Multiple Products Corp. div. of Miner Industries, Inc. (NYC) 1968; A. D. Sutton & Sons (NYC) 1970-72 and Vanity Fair Electronics Corp. (Brooklyn, NY) plastic figure with sound, 1955-56.

F6000 FIGURES — PORCELAIN BISQUE

Porcelain bisque figures are made of a special clay. The "green ware" from the mold is generally fired in a kiln just once before painting. If a glaze were applied after painting and the piece fired again, it would be procelain ceramic. The paint on early bisque figures had no protection and often flaked or wore off easily. Truly mint specimens are rare. Miniature bisque figure and candy stocking stuffers once sold for a penny. A pair of 6" Mickey and Minnie bisques with movable arms wholesaled for 80¢ per dozen pairs or 3¢ each. The retail was probably 5¢ to 10¢ for the pair. A mint pair today would sell for close to $1,000. New Grolier Enterprises limited edition (15,000) bisque figures sold for over $50. Capodimonte of Italy produced individual figures and limited editions scenes from animated features that sold for over $1,500. There have been hundreds of bisque figures in between. These have been made in two periods: 1931-41 and 1971-present. George Borgfeldt imported figures from Mickey cartoons, Silly Symphonies, Snow White and the Seven Dwarfs (in four sizes), Ferdinand the Bull and Pinocchio. Walt Disney Distributing Co. commissioned bisque figures starting in 1971. Most were sold at theme parks, but for a couple of years some special figures were marketed through gift ware dealers. These are marked "Disney Gift-Ware" with an image of Mickey with a paint brush. Foil seal identifying "UCGC-Taiwan" as the maker also appeared on the bottom of some pieces. Original art for this series has been sold at collector shows. Few of the early Borgfeldt bisque figures were advertised. The list below would not be as complete if it weren't for a couple special people the author wishes to acknowledge. This section has been compiled in cooperation with Bernie Shine and *Collectors' Showcase* magazine. A substantial number of the descriptions and color photos accompanying this classification originally appeared in *Collectors' Showcase* articles titled "Early Disney Bisque Figures Part I (Nov/Dec '84) and Part II (Mar/Apr '85) by Bernie Shine. Use of this copyrighted material has been granted by both the author, Bernie Shine and co-publisher Keith Koanis. The first number in parenthesis is the height of the figure in inches; the second, if any, the incised number found on the bisque near the copyright notice (also incised). SFTBH is an abbreviation for Single Figure Toothbrush Holder. Other manufacturers listed if not first period Borgfeldt or 70's Walt Disney Distributing Co. See color pages for illustrations of most bisque figures.

F6001	Bulbous head (4-3/4) 2 moveable arms, believed first	300 - 1000
F6002	Mickey (1-1/4) waving right hand, smallest Mickey bisque	25 - 75
F6003	Mickey (1-1/2) waving right hand	25 - 75
F6004	Mickey (1-3/4) right hand at hip; left at side	25 - 75
F6005	Mickey (1-7/8 x 3-1/4) riding in canoe	50 - 250
F6006	Mickey (2-3/4) two moveable arms	65 - 175
F6007	Mickey (2-3/4, S504) hands on hip	10 - 35
F6008	Mickey (2-3/4, S442) sitting position (Also see F6009)	10 - 45
F6009	Complete Mickey/Minnie tea set (includes F6009 & F6086 plus table, 2 chairs and miniature china set)	100 - 500
F6010	Mickey (3-3/4, S15) holding flag in right hand, sword on left	15 - 45
F6011	Mickey (3-1/4, S16) holding sword in right hand	10 - 40
F6012	Mickey (3-1/4, S17) holding rifle, wearing ammo packs, head slightly to right	15 - 45
F6013	Mickey (3-1/4, S429) holding rifle	10 - 35
F6020	Mickey (2-3/8, S26?) baseball glove on left hand	15 - 37
F6021	Mickey (2-3/8) baseball glove on left hand, ball in right	15 - 37
F6022	Mickey (2-3/8) holding baseball bat	15 - 45
F6023	Mickey (2-3/8) with catcher's gear and mit	15 - 45
F6024	Mickey (3-1/4, S64) baseball glove on left hand	15 - 45
F6025	Mickey (3-1/4, S65) baseball glove on left hand, ball in right	15 - 40
F6026	Mickey (3-1/4, S66) holding baseball bat	15 - 40
F6027	Mickey (3-1/4, S67) with catcher's gear and mit	15 - 40
F6030	Mickey (3-1/4) bulbous figure with conductor's baton, 2 moveable arms, white feet	20 - 60
F6031	Mickey (3-1/4) bulbous figure with song book, white feet	20 - 60
F6032	Mickey (3-1/4) bulbous figure playing accordian, white feet	20 - 60
F6033	Mickey (3-1/4) bulbous figure playing banjo, white feet	20 - 60
F6034	Mickey (3-1/4) bulbous figure playing French horn, white feet	20 - 60
F6035	Mickey (3-1/4) bulbous figure playing drum, white feet	20 - 60
F6040	Mickey (3-3/4, C72) playing snare drum	15 - 35
F6041	Mickey (3-3/4, C73) playing French horn	15 - 35
F6045	Mickey (3-3/4, S1390) nodding head attached to body with cord	35 - 200
F6047	Mickey (3-3/4, S177) wearing hat, holding cane	15 - 50
F6048	Mickey (4, S33) wearing hat, holding cane	15 - 50

BORGFELDT'S BISQUE NOVELTIES
of Mickey Mouse—Minnie Mouse and The Three Little Pigs

The American public has established an amazing demand for these miniature Bisque dolls of the Disney Characters. Children, of course, can't get enough of them to play with and grown-ups are calling for them to be used as favors, bridge prizes and sophisticated decorative touches for the living room, sun room and den. Any store showing this line in several departments will re-order constantly.

Write for full particulars

GEO. BORGFELDT CORPORATION
Licensee
44-60 East 23rd Street   New York, N. Y.

F6000

F6215   F6257   F6210

45

Multiple Character Porcelain Bisque Figurines

0553-9044 Snow White

0553-9043 Alice in Wonderland

0553-9045 Mickey & Minnie

0553-1776 Spirit of '76

0553-9046 Mickey & Pluto

0553-9053 Brer Bear

0553-9052 Lady & Tramp

0553-9505 Bambi & Friends

Not Shown Individual Characters
0553-9506 Bambi 4"
0553-9507 Flower 3"
0553-9508 Thumper 3"

F6271   F6273   F6270

Decorative Gifts

4" Porcelain Bisque Figurines 0553-9118 Spring 6 Piece Assortment

0553-9092 Mickey Riding Bike   0553-9106 Minnie Golfing   0553-9088 Donald Golfer

0553-9090 Donald At Beach

0553-9091 Mickey Tennis   0553-9089 Mickey D   0553-9104 Minnie Tennis

0553-9087 Mickey with Kite   0553-9086 Mickey on Ski   0553-9108 Daisy Skating   0553-9085 Mickey on Sled

0553-9099 Minnie Valentine   0553-9107

0553-9094 Donald Football   0553-9100 Minnie Blossom   0553-9101 Minnie Archer

4" Porcelain Bisque Figurines 0553-9120 Fall 6 Piece Assortment

0553-9078 Mickey Golfer   0553-9082 Goofy Baseball

0553-9301 Sir Hiss

0553-9303 Prince John   0553-9305 Robin Hood   0553-9083 Goofy Hockey

0553-9081 Goofy Surfing

0553-9080 Donald Fishing   0553-9079 Mickey Football

6" Character Porcelain Bisque Figurines

WALT DISNEY DISTRIBUTING CO.
General Office: P.O. Box 40, Lake Buena Vista, Florida 32830
(305/828-2411)

PRINTED IN U.S.A.   ©1976 WALT DISNEY PRODUCTIONS

DISNEY CLASSICS

F6049	Mickey (4) in tuxedo, holding top hat and cane	15 - 55
F6050	Mickey (4, S1277) wearing nightgown	8 - 20
F6652	Mickey (4-1/2, A567) standing next to garbage can	25 - 100
F6053	Mickey (5-1/4) standing on green platform, hands on hip	30 - 160
F6054	Mickey (5-1/4, A116 hands on hips	30 - 160
F6060	Mickey (5) SFTBH, bulbous head, moveable right arm (straight)	35 - 190
F6061	Mickey (5) SFTBH, head to left, moveable right arm (straight)	35 - 190
F6062	Mickey (5, C103) SFTBH, head to left, moveable right arm (slightly curved)	35 - 190
F6063	Mickey (5) two moveable arms	30 - 180
F6064	Mickey (5-3/4, C106) two moveable arms	30 - 180
F6068	Mickey (5-1/4) playing accordion	15 - 80
F6069	Mickey (5-1/4) playing French horn	15 - 80
F6070	Mickey (5-1/4) playing banjo	15 - 80
F6071	Mickey (5-1/4) playing drum	15 - 80
F6072	Mickey (5-3/4, S36) playing French horn	15 - 80
F6079	Mickey (7-1/2, S509) standing on green base, two moveable arms	200 - 675
F6080	Mickey (8-3/4) standing on green base, two moveable arms, largest Mickey bisque	250 - 850
F6085	Minnie (2-3/4, S505) hands on hip	10 - 35
F6086	Minnie (2-3/4, S443) sitting position (Also see F6009)	10 - 45
F6087	Minnie (3-1/4, S18) holding nurse's kit in right hand next to right leg, left hand on chest	15 - 50
F6088	Minnie (3-1/4, S493) holding nurse's kit under right arm, left hand on hip	15 - 50
F6090	Minnie (3-1/2, C69) playing mandolin	12 - 35
F6091	Minnie (3-1/2, C71) playing accordion	12 - 35
F6092	Minnie (3-1/2, S424) pushing wheelbarrow, used as pincushion	75 - 225
F6094	Minnie (3-1/4, S178) wearing hat, holding umbrella and purse	12 - 45
F6095	Minnie (4, S34) wearing hat and holding umbrella and purse	15 - 50
F6096	Minnie (4, S1276) wearing nightgown	8 - 20
F6097	Minnie (5) standing next to garbage can	25 - 100
F6100	Minnie (5) standing on green platform, hands on hips	30 - 160
F6101	Minnie (5-1/4, A117) hands on hips	30 - 160
F6102	Minnie (5) SFTBH, bulbous head movable right arm (straight)	35 - 210
F6104	Minnie (5) SFTBH, head turned right, left arm moveable (straight)	35 - 210
F6105	Minnie (5-1/4, C104) SFTBH head turned right, left arm moveable (slightly curved)	35 - 210
F6106	Minnie (5-3/4, S3?) playing violin	15 - 50
F6109	Minnie (5) two moveable arms	30 - 190
F6110	Minnie (6, C105) two moveable arms	30 - 190
F6120	Pluto (3-1/4, S433) seated next to guard house	20 - 80
F6121	Pluto (2-1/4) sitting position	10 - 40
F6122	Pluto (2-3/4, S35) sitting position	10 - 40
F6130	Donald (1-3/4, M-1) head turned to right, hands on hip	25 - 75
F6131	Donald (3, 3) bill open, hands at sides	15 - 50
F6135	Donald (3-1/4, S1333) holding flag	15 - 45
F6136	Donald (3, S1334) holding bugle	15 - 45
F6137	Donald (3, S1335) holding rifle	15 - 45
F6138	Donald (3, S1336) holding sword	15 - 50
F6140	Donald (3-1/4) walking, bill in air	15 - 50
F6143	Donald (3-1/4, 1) sitting on rocking horse	18 - 70
F6144	Donald (3-1/4, 2) sitting on scooter	18 - 70
F6145	Donald (3-1/4, 3) standing on scooter	18 - 70
F6147	Donald (3) in admiral's hat and coat	15 - 55
F6150	Donald (4, ??9) two moveable arms, medium bill	30 - 180
F6152	Donald (4-1/2, S1278) hands on hips	40 - 100
F6153	Donald (4) holding paintbrush and can of paint	50 - 150
F6155	Donald (4, S1158) playing mandolin	45 - 130
F6156	Donald (4, S1130) playing violin	45 - 120
F6157	Donald (4, S1131) playing accordion	45 - 120
F6158	Donald (4-1/2, S1130) playing violin	50 - 135
F6159	Donald (4-1/2, S1131) playing accordion	50 - 135

This pre-release photo of bisques from the animated feature Robin Hood showed 11 figures. Only Robin Hood, Sir Hiss, and Prince John were produced in quantity.

Small bisque series released in theme parks in 1976 where they were sold for over 10 years. Value 1 - 4 each.

47

Bisque and ceramic figures on sale at Disneyland in the summer of 1985.

Original art for a Disney Gift Ware figure.

RUBBER COMBINATION SETS
with Mickey Mouse, Big Bad Wolf and Three Little Pigs

Hot water bottle sets, doll sets, Disney Wolf and Pig sets are selling well.

Sets featuring the Three Little Pigs, and the Three Little Pigs with Big Bad Wolf are attractively packaged in boxes carrying colorful reproductions of the various characters.

Other combination sets are packed in boxes covered with pink color basket weave paper, very desirable for gift purposes.

The newness of this type of merchandise linked with the ever increasing popularity of Walt Disney subjects have skyrocketed these products into the field of big business. Display it in your windows frequently and advertise it regularly.

Write for full particulars

SEIBERLING LATEX PRODUCTS CO.
Licensee
Akron, Ohio   New York Office, 354 Fourth Ave.
Chicago Office—Merchandise Mart

F7000

MICKEY MOUSE, Pluto the Pup, the Three Little Pigs and the Big Bad Wolf are as famous in rubber as they are in motion pictures. Their sale is maintained and grosses more than a million units. Grown-ups want them as well as children—and the demand is one of the most consistent we've ever known. Each doll stands up—the Pigs are 6 inches high and the Wolf, 10 inches—all with removable heads—beautifully tinted with colors that are fast, crack-proof and water-proof. In stunning box sets or individual units, the Pigs being wrapped in cellophane. Stock these items and put them on your counters—you'll be amazed by the quantity you will sell.

Write for full particulars

SEIBERLING LATEX PRODUCTS COMPANY
Licensee
Akron, Ohio
New York Office: 354 Fourth Avenue   Chicago Office: Merchandise Mart

F7000

THREE LITTLE PIGS
in Rubber

These life-like creations developed a vast public demand overnight. They are irresistible to grown-ups as well as children. Furthermore, the dollar and cents volume is three times what you would usually expect as retail prices range up to 50c. per doll and $1.25 for the sets. The characters are of the standup type and each is 6' high. Movable heads offer added play value and appeal. Color decorations are not injurious in any way, they are fast and will not crack or run in water. Promote this line and you'll do much more than stimulate traffic—you'll give your sales and profit figures a big boost, too!

Write for full particulars

SEIBERLING LATEX PRODUCTS COMPANY
Licensee
Akron, Ohio   New York Office—354 Fourth Avenue
Chicago Office—Merchandise Mart

F7011

F6160 Donald (4-3/4) toothbrush holder, standing next to a pillar (See T6414)
F6162 Donald (5-1/4) toothbrush holder, profile of Donald looking right. (See T6115)
F6165 Donald (5-3/4, S1128) two moveable arms 180 - 700
F6175 The Goof (1-3/4) right hand in back, left hand to side 20 - 60
F6176 The Goof (3-1/2) right hand in back, left hand to side 15 - 30
F6177 Horace (1-7/8) hands to side 20 - 60
F6178 Horace (3-3/4) hands to side 15 - 30
F6179 Horace (5) arms folded across chest 30 - 80
F6183 Clarabelle (5) hands on dress 30 - 80
F6185 Mickey and Pluto (2-1/4) Mickey riding Pluto 15 - 45
F6186 Mickey and Donald (1-7/8 x 3-1/4) in canoe 35 - 150
F6190 Mickey and Pluto (5-1/2, S178) Mickey and Pluto side-by-side, Mickey's right arm moveable 55 - 170
F6192 Three Pigs, dancing, thimble base (3-1/2), each 8 - 18
F6193 Three Pigs, standing with instruments (3-1/2, S162, S165 and S?), each 6 - 18
F6194 Big Bad Wolf (1-3/4) 20 - 60
F6195 Big Bad Wolf (3-3/4) 10 - 22
F6200 Elmer Elephant (4-1/2, S1407) 2 moveable arms 35 - 100
F6201 Elmer Elephant (1-1/2) 10 - 30
F6210 Snow White (4 sizes, 2-1/4-6-1/2) standing 10 - 75
F6215 Dwarfs (4 sizes, 3-5) standing, each 5 - 15
F6257 Dwarfs with musical instruments (2-1/2), each 6 - 18
F6260 Ferdinand the Bull (1-3/4) 10 - 30
F6261 Ferdinand the Bull (3) 7 - 18
F6270 Pinocchio (6) 15 - 45
F6271 Pinocchio (3) or Figaro (2-1/2) 12 - 30
F6273 Honest John, Giddy, Geppetto or Jiminy Cricket (3) 10 - 28

Walt Disney Distributing Co. began in 1971 and ceased operations in 1977. Many of the bisque units designed and marketed by them were continued at theme parks. Items marked Disney Gift-Ware and not pictured were discontinued. Only three figures from the Robin Hood set were sold (Robin Hood, Prince John and Sir Hiss). The Spirit of '76 (See AMERICA ON PARADE) was sold mainly at Disneyland. Bea Jones, cast lead for the Disneyana Shop at the time, told the author only 429 of these pieces were sold. The popularity of bisque figures has prompted Grolier Enterprises to produce three different series based on 18 animated films — Magic Memories (limited to 15,000 @ $52.50 each), Musical Memories (limited to 19,950 @ $57.50 each) and Heroes and Villains (limited to 24,750 @ $57.50 each). Royal Orleans (United China & Glass Co.) have produced traditional and Christmas character bisques. Capodimonte of Italy has produced scenes depicting Snow White, Donald Duck and his nephews, Cinderella, Pinocchio, and Sleeping Beauty originally selling for 1000 - 2500 each. Individual pieces were made available for Snow White and the Seven Dwarfs and other scenes. A total of ten features are slated to be the subjects of Capodimonte bisques. Most of the theme park bisque designs as well as the Big Bad Wolf and individual music boxes featuring the Three Pigs, Mickey as conductor and Minnie playing the harp (all not shown) are kept in regular supply. New designs are being issued as well. Original art used to guide the manufacturer's sculptors has been selling for 30 - 40. This art normally consists of several views and one color overlay.

F7000 FIGURES — RUBBER

Seiberling Latex Products Co. (Akron) manufactured a line of solid (hard) and hollow rubber toys from 1934-42. The solid variety have survived well. Hollow rubber figures have mostly rotted. Sun Rubber Company (Barberton, OH) produced post-war rubber figures as did their Canadian counterpart, Viceroy Manufacturing Company, Ltd. Bayshore Industries, Inc. (Elkton, MD) produced foam rubber and "bend-me" figures from 1952 to 1962. Diener Industries, Inc. (Van Nuys, CA) made rubber "jigglers" and other figures 1968-72.

F7010 Big Bad Wolf 10 - 150
F7011 Three Pigs, each 8 - 75
F7020 Mickey, 6", full paint 25 - 150
F7021 Mickey, 6", black with highlight paint 35 - 180
F7022 Mickey, 3-1/2", black with highlight paint 15 - 55

F7010

F7034

F7000   F7022

F7041   F7040

F7030   F7021   F7020   F7022 F7032 F7025 F7026   F7049

F7054

F7000

THE SUN RUBBER COMPANY
BARBERTON, OHIO

F7067   F7066   F7068

lovable characters
from
WINNIE
THE
POOH
as featured by
WALT DISNEY
SOFT WASHABLE SAFE

HOLLAND HALL
PRODUCTS, INC.

Vinyl
squeeze
toys.
$1.00 each

Pooh
#81140

Kanga
& Roo
#81141

Tigger #81143   Eeyore #81142   Contact: Bryce Holland, 12 Magee, Stamford, Conn.

50

F7025	Donald, 6", movable head	25 - 150
F7026	Donald, 5", movable head	25 - 150
F7027	Donald, 6", squeeze toy	20 - 100
F7030	Pluto, 7" wide, red or yellow	5 - 40
F7032	Pluto, 3-3/8" wide, red or yellow	3 - 25
F7034	Elmer Elephant	5 - 60
F7040	Snow White	35 - 250
F7041	Seven Dwarfs, each	8 - 30
F7049	Ferdinand the Bull	5 - 20
F7050	Pinocchio	10 - 50
F7051	Jiminy Cricket	8 - 45
F7052	Figaro or Cleo, each	7 - 40
F7054	Donkey	8 - 45
F7065	Mickey (Sun Rubber) 1949	5 - 25
F7066	Donald (Sun Rubber) 1949	5 - 25
F7067	Pluto (Sun Rubber) 1949	4 - 20
F7068	Thumper (Sun Rubber) 1949	4 - 20
F7080	Bayshore foam rubber figures, each	5 - 30
F7090	Diener "jigging dolls", each	1 - 4

F7200 FIGURES — WOOD

George Borgfeldt & Company (NYC) sold wood Mickey and Minnie figures in 1931. Pluto figures followed in 1934, Donald in 1935 or 36 and Pinocchio in 1940. Bert B. Barry (Chicago) made non-Disney looking Pinocchio figures in 1940-41.

F7205	Mickey with lollypop hands	70 - 550
F7207	Mickey with disc hands	100 - 700
F7210	Mickey or Minnie, knob hands, 4", each	15 - 75
F7212	Mickey or Minnie, 4 finger hands, 5", each	35 - 100
F7214	Mickey or Minnie, 4 finger hands, 8", each	50 - 175
F7220	Pluto, 3+" long with dog house	35 - 110
F7220	Pluto, 3+" long, only	15 - 50
F7221	Pluto, 5-1/2+" long	20 - 80
F7225	Donald, 3"	25 - 125
F7227	Donald, 5"	35 - 200
F7235	Pinocchio	15 - 75
F7250	Line-Mar Mickey, Donald or Pluto, each	10 - 60

Also see DOLLS, FISHER-PRICE and TOYS — WOOD.

F7090

WALT DISNEY DISTRIBUTING CO.
P. O. BOX 40, LAKE BUENA VISTA, FLA. 32830 · PH. 824-2222

Hollow rubber Seven Dwarfs issued with a 21" Vinyl Snow White doll c. late 50's.

F7207   F7205

7TH YEAR WITH BORGFELDT'S

SINCE 1928, Mickey Mouse and Geo. Borgfeldt Corp. have been "clicking" in every important American market. The magnetic appeal of Mickey Mouse has produced rapid turnover and steady profits for retailers handling our line.

Write for full particulars

GEO. BORGFELDT
CORPORATION
Licensee
44-60 East 23rd Street, New York, N. Y.

F7200

F7210

F7225

F7214

F7221 F7227

F7220 F7235

F7390

F7400

F7380

F7386

F7378

F7377 F7376 F7382 F7381 F7379 F7385 F7375

82PN 75BE 80BC

76TR 077BM 073PM

F7405

F7351 F7345 F7331 F7355 F7354 F7349
F7356

F7320

F7515

F7300 FIGURES — OTHERS

Carnival chalk statues, molded woodfiber Pinocchio figures from Multi Products (Chicago) 1940-42, metal figures from Lincoln Logs (Halsam-Chicago) 1938 and John Wright, Inc. (Wrightsville, PA) 1972-73 are included in this section.

F7320	Donald, long bill, about 8″, 3 variations, each	7 - 30
F7331	Mickey, 15″ or 8″	10 - 100
F7345	Snow White	5 - 22
F7346	Dopey	6 - 25
F7349	Ferdinand the Bull	6 - 25
F7351	Dumbo	6 - 28
F7354	Donald, standing, 12″	5 - 16
F7355	Donald, holding apple	5 - 20
F7356	Donald on barrel bank, 12″	6 - 25

Multi-Products (F7375-F7425)

F7375	Pinocchio 7″	10 - 45
F7376	Pinocchio, arms at side, 4-3/4″	6 - 22
F7377	Geppetto, standing, 5-1/2″	5 - 18
F7378	Geppetto, sitting on box, 9″	10 - 50
F7379	Jiminy Cricket, hand extended	5 - 20
F7380	Jiminy Cricket, hand on knee	5 - 20
F7381	Honest John	6 - 25
F7382	Giddy	5 - 22
F7385	Lampwick	4 - 16
F7386	Figaro	4 - 16
F7390	Miniature 2″ - 2-3/8″ versions of Pinocchio, Geppetto, Jiminy Cricket, Lampwick and Giddy, each	5 - 20
F7400	Figural plaques, 3 versions, each	10 - 50
F7405	Figures used on paperweights, bookends, brush holders or pen holders, each	10 - 40
F7425	Figures as trophies, each	6 - 32
F7450	Dopey or Doc, Lincoln Logs, metal	15 - 35
F7452	Dopey and Sneezy salt & pepper, Lincoln Log set	25 - 60
F7458	Mickey holding flag, cast iron paperweight	2 - 8

Also see — SOAP, DOLLS and CHRISTMAS ORNAMENTS.

F7500 FILMS, SLIDES AND VIEWERS

Recreating the Disney film magic in the home has been the inspiration of a wide variety of home movies, film strips, slides and accompanying viewers. Hollywood Film Enterprises (Hollywood) distributed 16mm films (some sound) 1932-43, 8mm films 1944-50, and slides (1947). Tru-Vue and View-Master are noted for 3-D images. The Craftsmen's Guild made the most popular film strip viewer, besting many that preceded it. Hollywood Film Ent. product came in 25′, 50′, 100′, 200′ and 400′ black and white abridged versions of popular cartoons. Titles were usually different than theatrical versions. 16mm sound films are still collected, but boxes for the silent versions maintain the most interest. The cartoons are mostly available on video tape or disc, and the majority of old film is brittle or otherwise unshowable. Regular 8 and Super 8 (many sound) were very popular for over 30 years.

Hollywood Films and boxes 1932-1950 (F7510-F7520)

F7510	Safety film, Mickey with projector, boxed	5 - 20
F7515	Mickey Mouse Films, 16mm or 8mm	4 - 20
F7518	Walt Disney Character Films, 16mm or 8mm	4 - 15
F7520	Walt Disney Cartoons, 16mm or 8mm	3 - 15
F7522	Mickey Mouse "Safe Toy" films, each	2 - 10
F7525	Hollywood Movie Viewer and film loops	15 - 65
F7526	Extra character film loops (8) for F7525, each	1 - 3
F7528	Funnee Movee viewer and films (Irwin)	5 - 35
F7529	Extra character films for F7528, each	1 - 5
F7530	Craftsmen's Guild viewer and film	5 - 50
F7531	Extra character films (13) for F7530, each	1 - 5
F7532	35mm color slide sets (6) (Hollywood) 1947, each	5 - 20
F7534	Walt Disney Characters Tru-Vue viewer and filmstrip	4 - 24
F7535	Extra character filmstrips for F7534	1 - 3
F7536	Mickey Mouse viewer and 12 films	2 - 12
F7540	View-Master sets (depending on age)	5 - 30
F7541	View-Master reels in illustrated envelope	2 - 10
F7542	Tru-Vue 3-D card viewer and 1 card set	3 - 20
F7543	Extra character view card sets for F7542	2 - 10
F7544	Magic Eyes Story sets for F7542, each	2 - 10

F7510   F7520

F7518

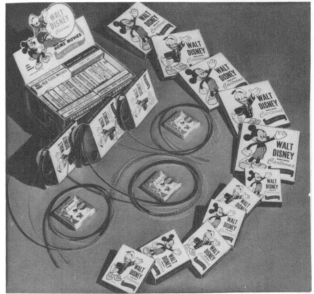

F7526

F7525

F7522

F7532

F7530

F7531

F7534

F7541

F7550

F7544

F7535

F7529

F7528

F7580

F7640

F7610

54

F7550 GE Show 'n Tell film strips and records, each   1 - 5

Licensed manufacturers — Action Films, Inc. (Mountain View, CA) hand operated 8mm viewer and cartridges, 1970-74; Automatic Toy Company (Staten Island, NY) toy TV sets, 1952-53; GAF Corporation (Portland, OE) Sawyer division, 1968-70, Tru-Vue division 1950-55, 68-71, View-Master division 1950's-82; Hollywood Film Enterprises (Hollywood) 1932-50; Irwin Corp. (Fitchburg, MA) 1949-51; W. C. Jones Publishing Company (LA) 1968, 70-71; Melton Industries (El Segundo, CA) 1953-56; Montron Corp. (Mountain View, CA) 1975-77; Telemovie Co. (Hollywood) 1932 and Viewmaster International Corp. (Portland, OR) 1982-84.

Also see FISHER-PRICE TOYS and PROJECTION EQUIPMENT.

F7580 FILM RENTAL AND SALES CATALOGS

Walt Disney Productions established a home entertainment division in 1952. They have issued catalogs on more or less a yearly basis. These interest a small number of home movie collectors and are valued at 1 - 5 each.

F7600 FISHER-PRICE TOYS

Fisher-Price (East Aurora, NY) manufactured wooden pull toys with printed paper laminated sides from 1935-1958. During this time they also made Donald Duck and Pluto paddle puppets. The company was also licensed for the years 1963-64 and produced 8mm cartridge movie viewers from 1975 - 84. In addition, talking books were introduced during this time.

F7612

F7610	Mickey/Pluto drum and cymbal	30 - 150
F7612	Donald/Pluto cart	20 - 120
F7613	Walking Donald carting Mickey's nephews	20 - 120
F7614	Long bill Donald flapping wings	8 - 45
F7618	Carnival with Donald, Pluto, Elmer and Mickey	20 - 120
F7620	Easter Parade with Donald, Clara Cluck & 3 Bunnies	20 - 120
F7630	Pluto paddle puppet	5 - 25
F7631	Donald paddle puppet	20 - 100
F7635	Bass drum and cymbal Mickey	15 - 75
F7636	Mickey Choo Choo	8 - 35
F7637	Short bill Donald with flapping arms	8 - 25
F7638	Donald (profile) xylophone	20 - 80
F7640	Doc and Dopey hammering drum	15 - 65
F7644	Struttin' Donald Duck	20 - 95
F7645	Mickey xylophone (solid black oval eyes)	15 - 70
F7647	Plucky Pinocchio (on donkey)	15 - 60
F7648	Pinocchio express (cart)	20 - 85
F7649	Donald Duck drum major	8 - 30
F7650	Same as F7649 with cart	10 - 40
F7655	Dumbo circus car	15 - 50
F7670	Donald Duck Choo Choo	8 - 35
F7671	Donald Duck cart (pupil eyes)	8 - 28
F7672	Mickey Mouse or Donald Duck drummer	5 - 24

F7613   F7614

F7618   F7630

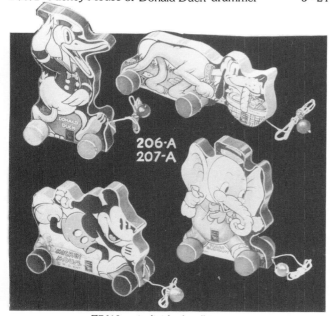

F7618 as individual pull toys.

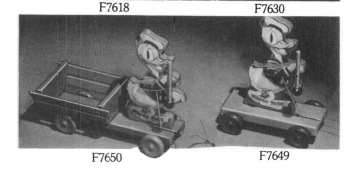

F7650   F7649

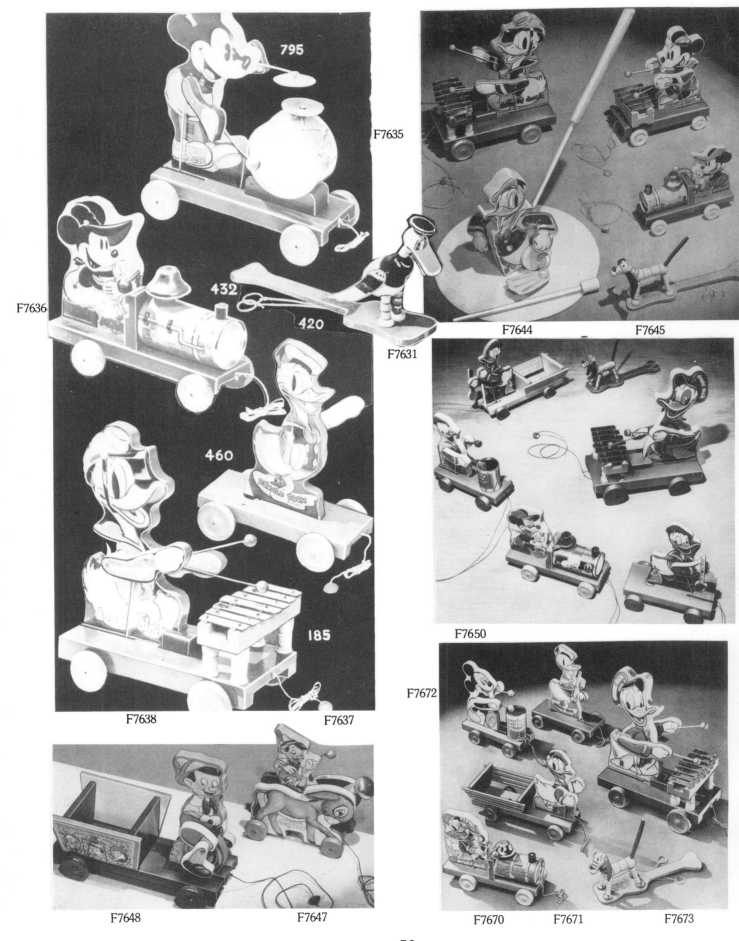

795

F7635

F7636

432

420

F7631

460

185

F7638   F7637

F7644   F7645

F7650

F7672

F7648   F7647

F7670   F7671   F7673

56

F7673	Donald xylophone (pupil eyes, 3/4 head view)	8 - 48
F7678	Donald with plastic feet and paper on all surfaces	5 - 24
F7679	Mickey Policeman on Motorcycle	5 - 24
F7682	Mickey Mouse puddle jumper	4 - 20
F7700	Cartridge film viewer	1 - 12
F7701	Extra film cartridges for F7700, each	1 - 6

F7750 FISHING TACKLE KITS

The Hamilton Metal Products Co. (Hamilton, OH) made four different fishing kits in 1935-36. ZEBCO division of Brunswick Corp. (Tulsa, OK) was licensed to make rods, reels and tackle boxes 1982-84.

F7751	Mickey Mouse fishing kit (small red box) 1935	10 - 60
F7752	Mickey Mouse fishing kit (large red box) 1935	15 - 80
F7753	Mickey Mouse fishing kit (small, with illustrated sides) 1936	10 - 50
F7754	Mickey Mouse fishing kit (large, with illustrated sides) 1936	15 - 70

F7800 FLASHLIGHTS

U. S. Electric Manufacturing Corp. (NYC) made illustrated flashlights 1935-38. Dan Brechner and Co. Inc. (NYC) imported similar "D" battery lights in 1961-63. Bantamlite Inc. (NYC) produced character and Disneyland pocket novelty flashlights (1955-59). Precision Specialties, Inc. (LA) 1945-52 made a plastic Pluto figural model. Shelbud Products Corporation (New Rochelle, NY) was licensed in 1972. Theme park designs have been continuously available without manufacturer credit.

F7810	Big Bad Wolf (USA lite)	6 - 45
F7811	Donald Duck (USA lite)	7 - 50
F7812	Elmer Elephant (USA lite)	6 - 45
F7813	Mickey Mouse (USA lite)	8 - 55
F7820	Pluto figural (Precision)	6 - 40
F7825	Bantamlites	1 - 8
F7835	Dan Brechner metal models	3 - 20
F7850	Theme park pocket or pen lights	1 - 3

F7752

F7751

F7885 FLOUR AND FEED SACKS

Packaging flour and feed in reusable textile sacks was a common practice from the Depression 30's to the early 50's. The empty bags were used by the farmer's wife as yardgoods to make clothing, curtains or whatever. Feed and seed merchants used them as incentives — the most wanted fabrics often made the sale. Texas Star Flour Mills (Galveston, TX) 1937-38 and Percy Kent Bag Co., Inc. (Kansas City, MO) 1949-53 were licensed to produce Disney character bags. The author is in the market to acquire samples to show in update editions of this book.

F7810

F7811

F7812

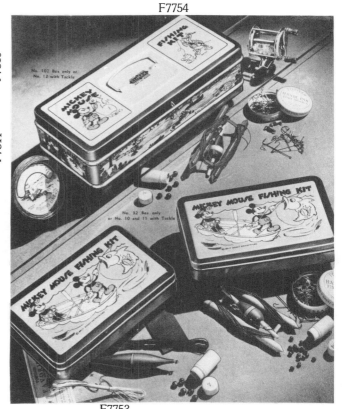

F7754

F7753

F7835

F7820

F7951 F7950 F7952

F8200

F8520

F7900 FLOWER VASES AND PLANTERS

Leeds China seems to have been the largest producer of these items (See L2500). Borgfeldt imported wall planters and Schumann sold some of the earliest vases. Modern day designs are mainly souvenirs produced for Disney theme parks.

F7910	Borgfeldt wall planter/vase	10 - 45
F7915	Schumann flower and bud vases, each	15 - 55
F7950	Mickey/Minnie	3 - 8
F7951	Cinderella or Snow White	3 - 8
F7952	Bambi, 3 styles, each	3 - 8

Licensed manufacturers- George Borgfeldt (NYC) 1930-39 (years for this product); Schumann China Corp. (NYC) 1932-34 and others.

Also see major ceramic makers listed at FIGURES — CERAMIC

F8200 FLIP MOVIES

There were a series of 12 premium flip movies given out by the first Mickey Mouse Club in 1932-33, value 10 - 50 each. Reproductions sell for 5 - 10. These were made by Moviescope Corporation (NYC). Dodge cars presented "Mickey Takes Minnie for a Ride" around 1934 worth 8 - 45. Theme parks produce flip movies at various times (valued at 1 - 3). Merrimack Publishing Corp. (NYC) has produced two-way, 4-color "Moving Picture Flip Books" in the 80's, worth 1 - 2 each.

F8500 FOOD AND DRINK PRODUCTS

This classification is intended to list food and drink products other than Donald Duck brands (See D8000). However, available information didn't permit positive identification and a substantial number of licensees listed are for years when Donald Duck Brands were strongest.

F8510	Mickey ginger ale and fruit drinks (Ludford) each	30 - 200
F8520	Mickey jam (Glaser Crandell) each	30 - 200
F8523	Opler cocoa malt flavoring	20 - 80
F8527	Canned evaporated milk (Morning)	4 - 32
F8533	Canned vegetables (Minnesota Valley)	2 - 20
F8535	Canned meats, beans and sausages (Whitson)	3 - 27
F8536	Canned corn, peas, etc. (Oconomowoc)	3 - 25
F8537	Frozen foods (Bucks County)	3 - 25
F8539	Preserves and jams (Phillips)	3 - 25
F8540	Mayonnaise, salad dressing and sandwich spreads, (Sar-A-Lee) each	3 - 25
F8548	Frozen fruits and vegetables (Godfrey)	2 - 20
F8549	Frozen fruits and vegetables (Keith)	2 - 20
F8550	Frozen fruits and vegetables (Lytle)	2 - 20
F8555	Frozen fruits and vegetables (Thomas)	2 - 20
F8561	Peanut butter jars and lids (Procter and Gamble)	1 - 12
F8565	Individual condiment servings (Sugar Foods) each	1 - 4
F8570	Jelly and ice cream topping gift sets (Charles)	1 - 8

Licensed manufacturers- Bucks County Frozen Products, Inc. (Doylestown, PA) 1949-51; Charlotte Charles, Inc. (Chicago) 1976-77; Glaser Crandell Co. (Chicago) 1934-36; Ben E. Keith Co. (Fort Worth, TX) 1953; E. R. Godfrey and Sons, Inc. (Milwaukee, WI) 1953; Ludford Fruit Products Company (Hollywood, CA) 1932-35; George Lytle, Inc. (St. Louis, MO) 1953; McLarens, Ltd. (Canadian) 1949-50; Minnesota Valley Canning Company (Minnesota Valley) 1947-48; Oconomowoc Canning Company (Oconomowoc, WI) 1949-50; E & A Opler, Inc. (Chicago) 1934-36; Phillips Products Corp. (San Francisco) 1949-54; Procter & Gamble (Cincinnati, OH); Sar-A-Lee Co. (Cleveland, OH) 1949-50; Sugar Foods Corp. (NYC) 1976; George H. Thomas, Inc. (Cincinnati, OH) 1953; and Whitson Food Products Company (Denton, TX) 1949-50.

Also see — BREAD WRAPPERS AND END SEALS; CANDY, CANDY BOXES AND WRAPPERS; CEREAL PACKAGES AND CUTOUTS; COOKIE BOXES AND PREMIUMS; DONALD DUCK PRODUCTS; ICE CREAM; and MILK BOTTLES.

F8600 FOOTWEAR — SLIPPERS, SOCKS, SHOES, ETC.

The boxes footwear came in would be more likely to catch a collectors' interest than the items themselves. Like apparel, footwear is not widely collected. Values are anybody's guess. There are many licensees, so this classification will be handled like APPAREL in Volume One — listing company, items licensed and year(s).

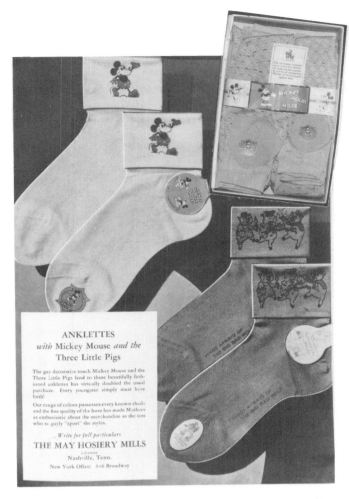

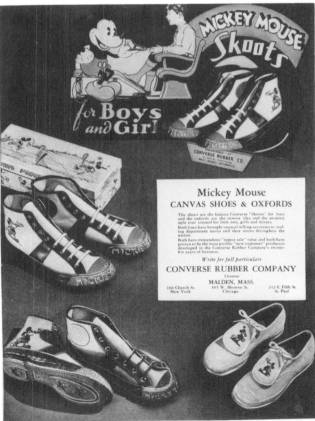

F8600

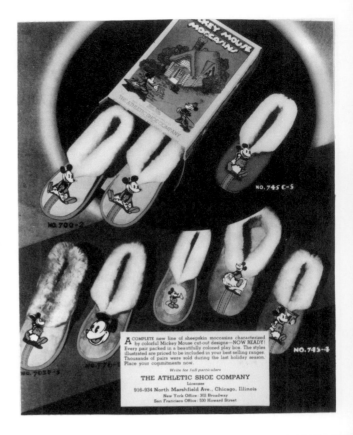

A COMPLETE new line of sheepskin moccasins characterized by colorful Mickey Mouse cut-out designs—NOW READY! Every pair packed in a beautifully colored play box. The styles illustrated are priced to be included in your best selling ranges. Thousands of pairs were sold during the last holiday season. Place your commitments now.

Write for full particulars

THE ATHLETIC SHOE COMPANY
Licensee
916-934 North Marshfield Ave., Chicago, Illinois
New York Office: 303 Broadway
San Francisco Office: 530 Howard Street

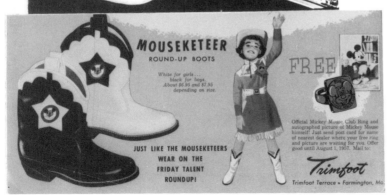

MOUSEKETEER ROUND-UP BOOTS

White for girls . . . black for boys. About $6.95 and $7.95 depending on size.

FREE

JUST LIKE THE MOUSEKETEERS WEAR ON THE FRIDAY TALENT ROUNDUP!

Official Mickey Mouse Club Ring and autographed picture of Mickey Mouse himself! Just send post card for name of nearest dealer where your free ring and picture are waiting for you. Offer good until August 1, 1957. Mail to:

Trimfoot
Trimfoot Terrace • Farmington, Mo.

F8600

F8600

Charlsam Footwear Corporation (Brooklyn, NY) 1939-40
  Slippers
Comfort Slipper Co. (Long Island City, NY) 1932
  Slippers
Continental Hosiery Corp. (NYC) 1947-56
  Children's hosiery (anklets and socks)
Converse Rubber Company (Malden, MA) 1933-44
  "Skoots" (gym shoes), canvas shoes and rubber boots
Elliot Knitwear Corp. (NYC) 1959
  Knitted slipper socks
Gold Seal Rubber Company (Boston) 1973-77
  Sneakers, rain and snow footwear
Herbert's Hosiery Mills, Inc. (NYC) 1938-39
  Children's hosiery
H. Jacob & Sons, Inc. 1938-39
  Slippers and shoes
Kayser-Roth Hosiery Co., Inc. (NYC) 1959
  Socks and stretch tights
Keepers Industries (Woodland Hills, CA) formerly Harrich Inc. 1972-84
  Men's/youth hosiery
Kusan, Inc. division of Bethlehem Steel Corp. 1973-84
  Roller and ice skates
Kushins, Inc. (Santa Rosa, CA) 1946-47
  Slippers and shoes
Lasting Impressions (Farmingham, MA) 1982-83
  Shoelaces
Maro Industries, Inc. (NYC) 1970-84
  Socks, hosiery, tights, leotards, head and wrist bands
Mart-Ray Manufacturing Co. (Brooklyn, NY) 1972-84
  Slippers, moccasins, sandals, slipper socks and baby shoes
May Hosiery Mills (Nashville, TN) 1932-36
  "Hosiery for boys, girls and children"
Morse Shoe Inc. (Canton, MA) 1977-84
  Sneakers, sandals, infants' footwear, boots and rubbers
Ripon Knitting Works (Ripon, WI) 1949-60
  Loafer sox with leather soles
Chester H. Roth Co. Inc. (NYC) 1952-56
  Children's anklets
Samsonite Corporation (Denver, CO) 1972
  Plastic indoor and outdoor skates
Savage Shoe Co., Ltd. (Canadian) 1949-50
  Children's shoes
Spartans Industries, Inc. (NYC) 1968-70
  Socks and hosiery
Sporting Shoe Company, Inc. (NYC) 1947-49
  Leather sandals, slippers, rubber boots and rubbers
Trimfoot Company, Inc. (Farmington, MO) 1949-58
  Slippers, sandals, shoes, cowboy boots and moccasins
Truitt Brothers, Inc. (Binghamton, NY) 1932-35
  Shoes
The Williams Manufacturing Co. (Portsmouth, OH) 1972-74
  Children's shoes

F9000 FRICTION TOYS

Friction motor toys filled a brief transition period in the 50's between wind-up and battery operated toys. A child would briskly run the toy on the floor without letting go. Then when the flywheel had the wheels spinning the toy was released to speed across a smooth surface floor. Louis Marx & Co., Inc. (NYC) and their Line-Mar brand were major sources for tin litho and plastic friction toys.

F9030	Donald's motorcycle (Line-Mar)	5 - 45
F9035	Thumper or Figaro (Line-Mar), each	3 - 12
F9038	Donald's rocket	5 - 45
F9100	Mickey Mouse racing kart (Marx)	5 - 50

F9100

F9038

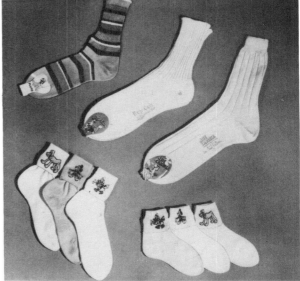

Kroehler figural furniture, the most collectible of the many Disney furniture makers.

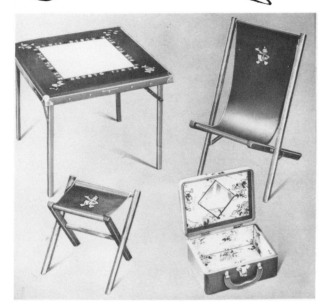

F9700

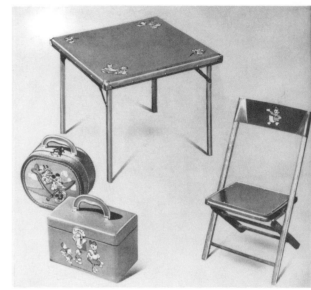

F9700

G1041

F9700

G1000

62

F9700 FURNITURE

Character furniture designs range from standard line table and chairs with a Mickey Mouse decal to the figural furniture made by Kroehler (Mickey rocker, clothes rack, chair and desk, plus Pluto bench, Minnie book end table and Clarabelle Cow shelves). Other furniture licensees and the products they made are listed below. Values are generally in the 3 - 35 range. Kroehler pieces bring 25 - 150.

Licensed manufacturers — American Toy and Furniture Co., Inc. (Chicago) 1956-57, wooden step chair, 1981-84, pegdesk, chests, clothes racks, night table and indoor play gym; Atlas Development Co, Ltd. (Richmond, CA) 1934-35, Kroehler Mickey Mouse furniture, additional pieces — crib, junior bed, tables, dresserrobe and treasure chest; Babcock Phillips (Richmond, VA) 1974-80, bean bag chair, pouf and building block hassocks; Brown, Jordan & Co. (El Monte, CA) 1972-74, patio chairs; Carolina Enterprises, Inc. (NYC) 1973-84, tables, chairs and desks; Chambers Belt Company (Phoenix, AZ) 1955-56 and 1984; Continental Cushion Spring Co. (Chicago) 1938-40, hassocks and chairs; Crawford Furniture Mfg. Co. (LA) 1934-35, chairs and stools; Creations for Children (Chicago) 1945-46, children's furniture and hassocks; Englander Co., Inc. (St. Paul, MN) 1973-84, mattresses, bunk and trundle beds and adult bedding; Fleischman Manufacturing Co. (NYC) 1944-46, Shoo-flys, table and chair sets; Gilbert and Ryan, Inc. (Racine, WI) 1984, director chairs; Hampden Speciality Products, Inc. (Easthampton, MA) 1956-57, metal folding table and chair set; Himalayan Pak Co., Inc. (Monterey, CA) 1957-59, child's aluminum frame canvas chairs; Ideal Toy Corp. (Hollis, NY) 1968-82, inflatable furniture; Kroehler (see Atlas Development); Kusan, Inc. (Nashville, TN) 1973-84, table and chair sets; Ladd Industries (High Point, NC) 1982, juvenile furniture; Lea Industries division of S & H Furniture Co., Inc. (High Point, NC) 1981, juvenile furniture; Okla Homer Smith Furniture Mfg. Co. (Ft. Smith, AR) 1973-79, juvenile furniture and mattresses; The Mengel Company (St. Louis, MO) 1935-39, tables and chairs; Modern Kitchen Bureau (?) 1940-41, promoted electric water heaters; Neeval Manufacturing Co. (Kansas City, MO) 1949-56 folding tables and chairs; Relaxon Products (Chicago) 1940-41, chairs; Storkline Furniture Corp. (Chicago) 1938-41, juvenile furniture; Superior Bedding Co. (LA) 1945-48, mattresses; C. G. Wood Co. (Girard, PA) 1975, director chairs; and Zee Toys, Inc. (Long Beach, CA) 1983-84, inflatable furniture.

G1000 GAMES

Disney games have been broken down into seven classifications. Where there is duplication of licensees in these sub-classes, manufacturers are listed only once in this introductory section. Licensees that produced games limited to the subsections are listed at the individual class. Some game boxes were updated as animated features were re-released.

Licensed manufacturers for board games and/or games found at more than one sub-class — American Toy Works (NYC) 1938-41; AMSCO Industries, Inc., division of Milton Bradley (Warminster, PA) 1972; George Borgfeldt and Company (NYC) 1930-41; Einson-Freeman Co. (Long Island City, NY) 1933-34, 38-39; Gardner and Company (Chicago) 1955; Johnson & Johnson (Tek toothbrush offer) 1938-39 and 1947-48; Kenilworth Press, Inc. (NYC) 1933-34; Marks Brothers Company (Boston) 1934-41, 46-48; Milton Bradley Company (Springfield, MA) 1931-42, 72-79; ONTEX-Ontario Textiles Ltd. (Canadian) 1949-50; Parker Brothers (NYC) 1933-41, 47-55, 68-84; Transogram Company, Inc. (NYC) games 1952-55, 68-71 and Whitman Publishing Company (Racine, WI) games 1939, 1952-84.

G1001 GAMES — BOARD

G1010	Mickey Mouse Coming Home Game (Marks) 2 sizes	20 - 80
G1011	Mickey Mouse Scatter Ball (Marks)	20 - 80
G1012	The Game of Who's Afraid of the Big Bad Wolf? (Marks)	15 - 75
G1015	Walt Disney's Own Who's Afraid of the Big Bad Wolf? (Parker)	12 - 50
G1016	Walt Disney's Own Game — The Pied Piper of Hamelin (Parker)	12 - 50
G1017	Walt Disney's Own Red Riding Hood (Parker)	12 - 50
G1020	Mickey/Minnie ball game #267 (Marks)	25 - 125
G1021	Mickey Mouse Circus Game also #267 (Marks)	25 - 125
G1030	The Game of Snow White and the 7 Dwarfs (MB)	10 - 45
G1031	Walt Disney's Own Game Snow White and the 7 Dwarfs (Parker)	10 - 45
G1032	Walt Disney's Game Parade (American Toy)	15 - 55
G1035	Walt Disney's Own Game Ferdinand the Bull (Parker)	10 - 45
G1036	The Game of Ferdinand the Bull in the Arena (Whitman)	15 - 55

G1011

G1042

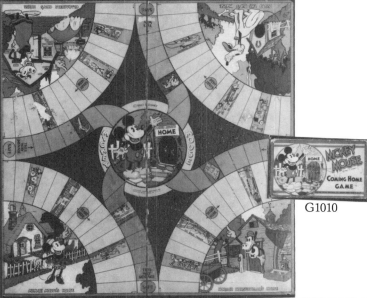

G1010

G1030

G1038

G1012

G1021

G1020

WALT DISNEY'S OWN
"Who's afraid of the
BIG BAD WOLF
GAME

G1015

G1040

WALT DISNEY'S
OWN GAME
FERDINAND the Bull

G1035

WALT DISNEY'S
Own Game
The Pied Piper of Hamelin

G1016

WALT DISNEY'S
OWN GAME
SNOW WHITE
and the 7 DWARFS

G1031

G1150

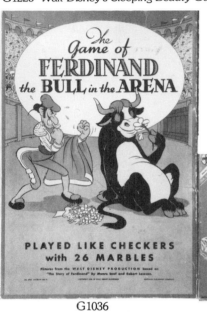

G1036

G1017

G1175

G1185

G1198

G1100

G1032

G1195

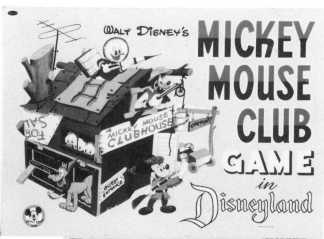

WALT DISNEY'S **MICKEY MOUSE CLUB GAME** *in Disneyland*

G1190

WALT DISNEY'S OFFICIAL **Frontierland** GAME

G1191

WALT DISNEY'S **ADVENTURELAND** GAME

G1192

WALT DISNEY'S **Fantasyland** Game

WALT DISNEY'S **TOMORROWLAND** ROCKET to the MOON GAME

Disneyland **RIVERBOAT** GAME

Disneyland **MONORAIL** GAME

G1200

WALT DISNEY'S **SLEEPING BEAUTY** Game

G1225

WALT DISNEY'S **Mary Poppins** GAME

WALT DISNEY *Sleeping Beauty Castle*

Walt Disney's **Donald Duck** MONEY BAG GAME *for the entire family*

WIN THE MOST MONEY BAGS FROM UNCLE $CROOGE'S MONEY BIN
2 to 4 Players

Other board games from the 60's and 70's. Value 1 - 10.

66

G2000 GAMES — CARDS

Mickey Mouse ice cream cones probably beat Whitman with the first card game. Whitman did adult bridge tally sets and regular playing card decks, as well as children's Old Maid and other card games. Russell Manufacturing Co. has been a major card game producer. Playing card collecting became a fad in the early 50's and a number of collector's trading cards were issued. Theme parks have been the source of an ever changing array of card decks.

G2005	Mickey Mouse Cones — imprinted with the names of dairies — an early Kay Kamen promotion	10 - 50
G2008	Card game from Post Toasties box	4 - 15

Whitman (G2010 thru G2035)

G2010	Mickey Mouse Old Maid (2 designs)	6 - 35
G2011	Mickey/Minnie Playing Cards	5 - 25
G2012	Mickey/Minnie bridge cards & tally set	8 - 45
G2013	Three Little Pigs playing cards	4 - 20
G2014	Three Little Pigs bridge tally set	8 - 45
G2015	Miniature Mickey Mouse playing cards	4 - 18
G2016	Clarabelle and Horace playing cards	5 - 25
G2020	Dopey playing cards — 2 deck set	5 - 25
G2021	Miniature Snow White playing cards	4 - 18
G2025	Pinocchio Playing Card Game	6 - 35
G2026	Pinocchio and Jiminy Cricket playing cards, set	5 - 25
G2035	Donald Duck Playing Card Game	5 - 35
G2050	War insignia trading cards, each	1 - 2
G2060	Mickey Mouse Library of Games (Russell)	8 - 40
G2067	Donald Duck Card Game (Whitman) 3 box designs	5 - 20
G2073	Mickey Mouse Canasta Junior (Russell)	5 - 20
G2080	Alice in Wonderland/White Rabbit bridge decks, set	12 - 24
G2090	Mickey Mouse Club card games (Russell) each	2 - 6
G2100	Disneyland collector's cards (12) Whitman, set	12 - 24
G2119	Disneyland Card Game (Whitman)	3 - 15
G2120	Disneyland playing card decks, each	2 - 10
G2150	Mickey Mouse Funny Rummy	1 - 6
G2160	Mary Poppins Card Game (Whitman)	1 - 8
G2164	Library of Games — 60's version	6 - 18
G2170	Ed-U-Cards, Mickey Mouse, Pinocchio, Jungle Book and others, each	1 - 5
G2190	Walt Disney World (Castle or miniatures) playing cards	1 - 4
G2195	Mickey Mouse round playing cards	2 - 10
G2196	Mickey Mouse Jumbo playing cards	1 - 6
G2197	Mickey playing cards, traditional or jester, each	1 - 3
G2199	Old Witch Card Game (2 versions) each	1 - 2

Licensed manufacturers — Ed-U-Cards (Commack, NY) 1968-78, became Binney & Smith, Inc., 1979-83; Kay Kamen (NYC) 1933-35 and Russell Mfg. Co. (Leicester, MA) 1945-55, 1968-84.

G2005   G2010   G2035

G2016

G2008   G2025

G2013

G2014   G2012

G2011

G2020

G2026

G2067

G2073

G2067

G2060

G2067

G2080

G2090

G2164

G2195

G2120

G2050

G2170

G2150

G2119

G2015

G2100

G2500 GAMES — EDUCATIONAL

There have been many educational materials with Disney characters including puzzle and teaching machine type games found at other classifications. A series of first learning games dealing with letters, numbers, colors, animals and friends were issued by Western Publishing Co. (Racine, WI) in the 60's. Value 1 - 8 each.

Also see — ALPHABETS, GAMES — ELECTRONIC and GAMES — PUZZLE

G2900 GAMES — ELECTRIC AND ELECTRONIC

These games are AC or battery operated. Atari also developed a game for home computers in 1983.

G2905	Mickey Mouse Funny Facts Game (Einson-Freeman)	25 - 250
G2930	Disneyland Electric quiz (Jacmar)	4 - 15
G2931	20,000 Leagues Under the Sea Electric Quiz (Jacmar)	4 - 15

G2160   G2199

G2190

G2197

G2500   G2500

G2500

G2930

G2931

G2938

G3030

G3020

G3005

G3040

G2932

G2905

G2932	Magic adder (MMC) Jacmar	4 - 12
G2933	Disneyland Electric Tours with Davy Crockett	5 - 25
G2938	Mickey Mouse Electric Treasure Hunt (Tudor)	6 - 30
G2950	TRON hand held electronic game (Tomy)	8 - 32

Licensed manufacturers — Atari, Inc. (Sunnyvale, CA) 1983-84; Jacmar Mfg. Co., Inc. (NYC) 1953-55; Nintendo of America, Inc. (Redmond, WA) 1983-84 LCD electronic games; Tomy Corp. (Carson, CA) 1982; and Tudor Metal Products Co. (Brooklyn, NY) 50's.

G3000 GAMES — PUZZLE

A number of Disney games mixed play action with puzzles. The popular Lotto games provided a race for young children to see who could get all the Disney character shapes into the correct openings first.

G3005	Walt Disney Jigsaw Lotto (Jaymar) 3 sizes	5 - 35
G3008	Character SCRAMBLE (Plane Facts)	5 - 35
G3020	Donald Comic Picture Puzzle (Parker)	4 - 20
G3030	Mickey Mouse Mix-Up-Game (Parker)	3 - 15
G3040	Mickey Mouse Pop 'N Play (Gabriel)	2 - 12

Licensed manufacturer — Gabriel Industries, Inc. division of CBS Toys (NYC) 1981-82; Jaymar Specialty Co. (NYC) 1943-84 and Plane Facts Co. (NYC) 1943-45.

G3200 GAMES — SKILL

Skill games are ones where motor practice can improve physical performance. Target, toss, pinball, table top sports and hand held games are included in this section.

G3210	On the Warpath shooting game (Borgfeldt) 1932	50 - 500

Marks Brothers Co. (G3225-G3244)

G3225	Bean Bag Game	15 - 60
G3226	Target (2 sizes)	15 - 85
G3228	Bagatelle	20 - 120
G3229	Hoop-La Game	20 - 100
G3230	Mickey Soldier set (18)	20 - 100
G3231	Pop Game	18 - 90
G3232	Hand held ball puzzle games (3), each	10 - 55
G3235	Topple-Over Shooting Game	12 - 70
G3236	Mickey Rollem Game	10 - 55
G3237	Mickey/Minnie Rollem Game	10 - 55
G3240	Snow White moving target	20 - 120
G3244	Mickey/Donald Soldier set (8)	8 - 50
G3248	Jacks set (U. S. Lock and Hardware)	4 - 25
G3249	Bow and arrow set (Wilson)	7 - 35
G3252	Dopey Bean Bag Game (Parker)	5 - 35
G3253	Donald Duck Bean Bag Game (Parker)	5 - 35
G3256	Mickey Ski Jump Target Game (American)	10 - 75
G3257	Snow White and the 7 Dwarfs Target Game (American)	10 - 75
G3260	Pinocchio ring toss (De-Ward)	4 - 25
G3280	Donald Duck Tiddley Winx (Jaymar)	3 - 18
G3290	Target set (Lido)	2 - 15
G3293	Donald Duck Pins (Pressman)	2 - 18
G3295	Mouskatennis (Pressman)	2 - 15
G3298	Mickey Mouse Basketball (Gardner)	3 - 20
G3299	Donald Duck Bean Bag Game (Gardner)	3 - 20
G3300	Casey Jr. Game (Gardner)	3 - 20
G3314	Mickey Mouse or Davy Crockett target sets (Daisy)	3 - 20
G3315	Davy Crockett bow and arrow set (Withington)	3 - 20
G3316	Davy Crockett bow gun (Withington)	3 - 20
G3320	Disneyland Dipsy Doodles, 3 designs, each	1 - 5
G3330	Tiddly Winks (Whitman)	2 - 10
G3331	Ludwig Von Drake Tiddly Winks (Whitman)	2 - 10

Licensed manufacturers — Daisy Manufacturing Co. (Plymouth, MI) 1955-59; De-Ward Novelty Co. (Angola, NY) 1939-41; Lido Toy Company (NYC) 1954-55; Northwestern Products Co. (St Louis, MO) 1957-59, bagatelle, pinball and spin games; Pressman Toy Corp. (NYC) 1955-59; Synergistics Research Corp. (NYC) 1979-83, velcro target games; U. S. Lock and Hardware Co. (Columbia, PA) 1934-40; Rollin Wilson Co. (Memphis, TN) 1936-37 and Withington, Inc. (West Minot, ME) 1955-57.

G3500 GAMES — OTHER

This miscellaneous group includes traditional games like dominoes, bingo and pin the tail on Mickey to Whizzer wheel and magic printing machine games.

G3520	Mickey Mouse Dominoes (Halsam)	15 - 60

G3320

G3005

G3210

G3228

G3226

G3237

G3226

G3231

G3230

G3244

G3225

G3240

G3229

G3260

G3252 G3256 G3257

G3299

G3253

G3295

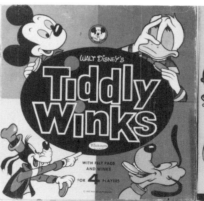

G3298

G3280

G3293

G3235

1937 Marks Brothers Merchandise Catalog ad.

G3330 G3331

G3290

G3520

G3543 Whizzer Wheel (Ideal)   5 - 25

G3540

G3545   G3535   G3525

G3570

G4083

G4980

G4070

G3525	Mickey Mouse Party Game (Pin the Tail)	10 - 40
G3526	Same as G3525 but in box (Marks Bros.)	10 - 55
G3530	Pin the Nose on Pinocchio (Parker)	6 - 30
G3535	Picture Dominoes (Transogram)	5 - 25
G3540	Double Dominoes	4 - 22
G3545	Bingo (Lido)	4 - 20
G3550	Magic Printing Machine Game (Norstar)	3 - 15
G3570	Pin the Tail on Mickey Mouse (Hallmark)	1 - 3

Licensed manufacturers — Hallmark (Kansas City, MO) 1972; Ideal Toy Corp. (NYC) 1955-57; Northstar Corp. (Bronx, NY) 1968 and Winthrop-Atkins Co., Inc. (Middleboro, MA) 1969-70, magnetic game.

G4000 GLASSES — DRINKING

Disney character premium tumblers were used to promote the sale of cottage cheese from 1933 to 1941 and 1947-48. There were main character, Snow White, Pinocchio and Disney All Star sets. Many of the one color glasses came in a variety of different colors and sizes. Bosco drink mix offered a special small size. Libbey Glass division of Owens-Illinois Glass Co. was the major producer. There was a multi-colored Snow White set also. Character glasses have been popular theme park souvenirs since Disneyland opened. The 70's gave rise to collector's sets of 3 to 8 glass tumblers issued by soft drink and fast food companies.

G4025   G4010

T9205

G4003	Mickey milk glass tumbler	5 - 50
G4005	Three Pigs glass breakfast set (Krueger) 1934	25 - 125
G4010	Main character cottage cheese premiums, Mickey, Minnie, Donald, Pluto, Clarabelle, Horace, Three Pigs, Elmer and Funny Bunny, each	3 - 15
G4025	Snow White & 7 Dwarfs premiums, each	3 - 12
G4033	Snow White & 7 Dwarfs, Bosco, each	5 - 20
G4034	Snow White & 7 Dwarfs, full color, set	35 - 70
G4048	Kraft Snow White Premium set	35 - 70
G4055	Disney All Star Parade series, 1939, each	5 - 15
G4070	Pinocchio premiums (12), each	5 - 15
G4083	Pinocchio glass promotion folder	5 - 35
G4099	Calox Pinocchio safedge glass (McKesson & Robbins)	
G4100	Character pair glasses, 40's — Mickey/Minnie, Donald/Daisy, Pluto/Goofy, Pinocchio/Jiminy Cricket, each	4 - 12
G4110	Cinderella set (8), each	2 - 5
G4120	Alice in Wonderland set (8), each	2 - 6
G4150	Character glasses, Disneyland souvenir	2 - 6
G4180	Procter & Gamble Sleeping Beauty set, each	3 - 9
G4220	Theme park character glasses	1 - 3
G4250	Coca-Cola character set (6), each	2 - 8

The promotional character collector's sets are often issued regionally. There are also variations from one fast food chain to another. Sets known include Mickey's 50th Birthday, The Rescuers, Mickey Mouse Club, Mickey Mouse Club with film borders, and Mickey's Christmas Carol. Values are generally 1 - 3 per glass.

Licensed manufacturers — Allied Plastics Co., Inc. (LA) 1949-53, plastic tumblers; Eldon Manufacturing Co. (LA) 1955; Federal Glass Company of Ohio (supplied glass tumblers to Canada Packers Ltd. for York Peanut Butter) 1955; Hazel-Atlas Glass Company (Wheeling, WV) 1959; Kraft-Phoenix Cheese Company (Set of Snow White and Seven Dwarfs tumblers for 8 lids from Parkay Margarine) 1938-39; Richard G. Krueger Co. (NYC) 1931-41; Libbey Glass Company division of Owens-Illinois Glass Co. (Toledo, OH) 1936-43, 49-52, 55-56, 77-80; Lily div. of Owens-Illinois (Toledo, OH) 1975, paper cups; McKesson & Robbins, Inc. (Calox Pinocchio safedge glass giveaway) 1940-41; Procter & Gamble (Cincinnati, OH) 1959; and U. S. American (LA) 1983-84.

G4220

G4900 GLASSES — EYE AND SUN

The first sunglasses on record were licensed in 1935 — prescription eyeglass frames in 1984. They have been more functional than collectible. Value 2 - 25 (Bachmann), others 1 - 4.

Licensed manufacturers — Bachmann Brothers, Inc. (Philadelphia, PA) 1935-36, 57-58; Comptone Co., Ltd. (NYC) 1955, 68; Golden Eagle Enterprises, Inc. (Selma, AL) 1984; Hudson Universal Ltd. (Englewood, NJ) 1984; M. R. Nadel Co. (NYC) 1970-71; Opto-Specs, Ltd. (NYC) 1972-75 then as Oculens, Ltd. (Oceanside, NY) 1976-83.

G4980 GLOBE OF THE WORLD

Rand McNally & Co. (Skokie, IL) made character world globes and a world globe game with magnetic characters in 1955. Globes alone are valued at 15 - 50, the games at 20 - 75.

G5000 GLOVES AND MITTENS

Gloves, mittens, and gauntlets might be more collectible if more

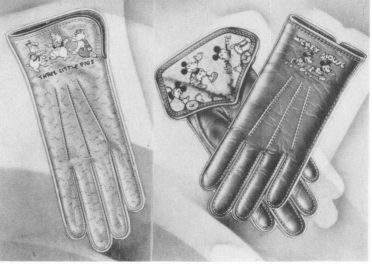

G5000

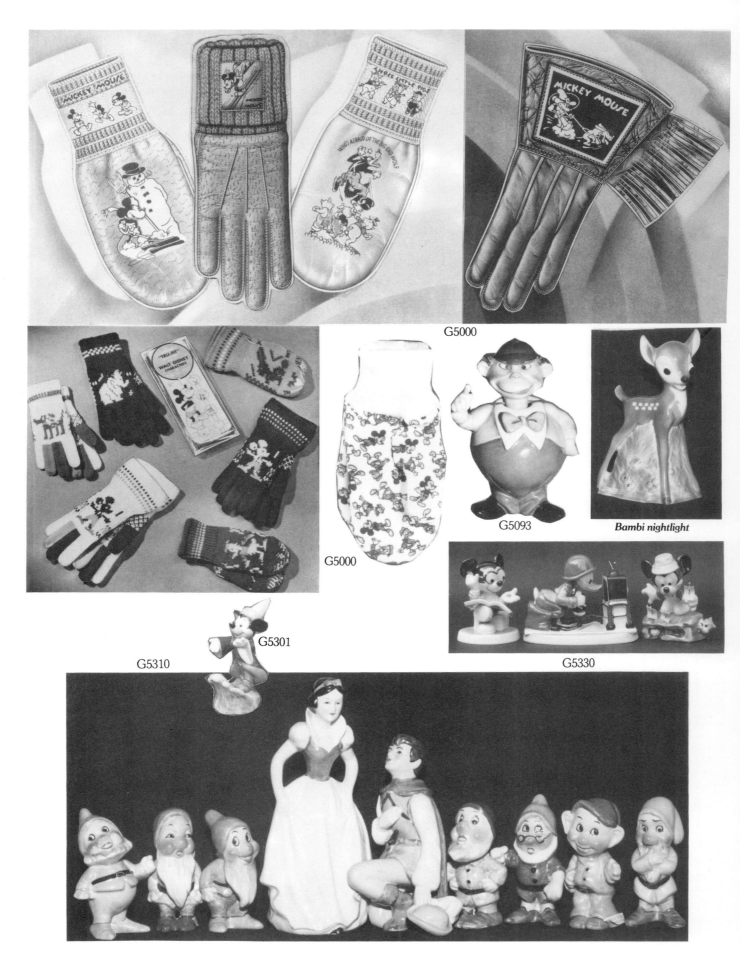

G5000

G5000

G5093

Bambi nightlight

G5310

G5301

G5330

76

of them were around. Eisendrath, in particular, produced some spectacular designs. These might fetch 50 - 75 in nice condition. Others are less exciting, 1 - 8 per pair, up to 20 for knitted-in designs.

Licensed manufacturers — Eisendrath Glove Company (Chicago) 1933-36; Franklin Tru-Fit Glove Co. (Chicago) 1946-59; Victor B. Handal & Bro., Inc. (NYC) 1983-84; Premire Gloves, Inc. (Johnstown, NY) 1976; Stadium Sport-Headwear Co. (NYC) 1939-40; Thornton Glove Co., Inc. (Totwa, NJ) 1972+ and Wells Lamont Corp. (Chicago) 1959, 68 and 70.

G5500 GOEBEL

Goebel, the German company famous for Hummel overglaze figurines, produced a continuous series of Disney figures from 1950-67. The Goebel 50th Anniversary book lists them as being sold in the U.S. from 1952-54; however, Ebeling & Reuss Co. (Philadelphia, PA; now Devon, PA) was licensed to import "Disney Hummel figures" as of Feb 24, 1955 for an undetermined period. The vast majority of the 220 pieces in the first series were based on the film Bambi. Many merely used the same figures on different bases, ashtrays, or in different scene groupings. The Goebel Disney figures sold in America had a "full bee" mark (a bee in the letter V) on the underside of each piece, along with the word "Germany." Two figures, Bambi and Mickey as the Sorcerer's Apprentice, were made for sale at theme park Disneyana shops in the late 70's. These and a new series of 10 figures are marked "Goebel." The "full bee" figures were painted in earthier tones and shading very close to Hummel figures. More modern figures are brighter with less shading. Value of "full bee" figures ranges from 35 for a small Bambi to several hundred for larger multi-figure scenes. The full bee set of Snow White and the Seven Dwarfs did not include the Prince. This piece was added in a later remake of the set. A third and smaller Snow White set was issued in 1984, also without a prince. Only one of Goebel's three U.S. distributors is responsible for importing the Disney line — Goebel United States (formerly Hummelwerk), a wholly-owned subsidiary of Goebel Art GmbH, West Germany, based in Pennington, NJ. The sculptors who modeled the original series included Arthur Moeller, Reinhold Unger, Karl Wagner with additional pieces being done by artists Aschermann, Wolf and Wehlte. Following is a complete list of Disney Goebel figures as recorded by the company. The specific character is not always listed nor the description too accurate from the German translations. Read rocking figures as nodders, and the term "lips" refers to the indentation for a cigarette on an ashtray. Figures found most often in the U. S. include Dumbo on the edge of the cliff, Elmer Elephant and Tillie the Tiger, Pinocchio, Honest John, Giddy and Figaro. These are all in the list somewhere, but positive identification still needs to be made on many pieces. The problem is complicated in that many figures might not have ever been sold in the U. S. Values other than the broad guidelines mentioned above are not possible at this time. The list is presented as it was received from Goebel for collector interest. The Goebel number is the last digit(s) of the Tomart number. Disney figures were numbered and each number was preceded by the letters DIS. The incised number is legible on some pieces. To determine exact Goebel identification, read G5001 as DIS 1; G5014A as DIS 14A.

G5001 Dwarf "Bashful" (1950)
G5002 Dwarf "Sleepy"
G5003 Dwarf "Happy"
G5004 Dwarf "Grumpy"
G5005 Dwarf "Sneezy"
G5006 Dwarf "Dopey"
G5007 Dwarf "Doc"
G5008 Sitting up rabbit as ashtray with lip on tail
G5009 Ashtray and Bambi
G5010 Standing deer and jumping rabbit on base
G5011 Standing Bambi without base
G5012 Standing girl "Snow White"
G5013A Larger deer with its head turned backwards, a butterfly is sitting on its tail
G5013B Small deer with its head turned backwards, a butterfly sitting on its tail
G5014A Small skunk sitting on its hind legs
G5014B Small standing skunk
G5015 Ashtray with two lips and a dressed duck in the

G5008   G5021   G5078

ash-bowl
G5016 Pig with hat "Seier Pig"
G5017 Little Indian "Hiawatha"
G5018 Sitting up rabbit beside a vessel
G5019 Standing rabbit beside a vessel
G5020 Standing duck beside a vessel
G5021 Lying Bambi without base
G5022 Standing deer on base with stem
G5023 Sitting rabbit, the ears are on the back
G5025 Sitting skunk with a flower in both its paws
G5026 Sitting laughing rabbit spreading out its paw
G5027 Owl sitting on a branch, with stem as vase
G5028 Owl spreading out its wings on tray with two lips
G5029 Flying owl with book as wall ornament
G5030 Owl of G5029 beside a vessel as wall-vase
G5031 Cigarette box, on its cover the deer of G5021
G5032 Rabbit of G5023 as salt shaker
G5033 Skunk of G5025 as salt or pepper shaker
G5034 Rabbit of G5026 as salt shaker
G5035 Bird sitting on a branch with its tail raised
G5036 Sitting rabbit with its forelegs hanging down
G5037A Owl sitting on stem, book-end
G5037B Rabbit sitting beside stem, book-end
G5038 Rabbit lying flat on face, hind legs spread out
G5039 Sitting rabbit, vessel on back
G5040 Rabbit of G5036 as salt shaker
G5041 Rabbit of G5039 as salt shaker
G5042A Stem and Bambi looking right, vase
G5042B Stem and Bambi looking left, vase
G5043 Sitting rabbit, hind legs stretched, foreleg raised
G5044 Bird sitting on branch, looking downward
G5045 Pig of G5016 as ashtray
G5046 Duck of G5020 as ashtray
G5047 Rabbit of G5019 beside round vessel, toothpick holder
G5048 Indian of G5017 beside round vessel, toothpick holder
G5049 Indian of G5017 as ashtray
G5050 Rabbit of G5024 as salt shaker
G5051 Dwarf of G5001 as vase
G5052 Dwarf of G5002 as vase
G5053 Dwarf of G5003 as vase
G5054 Dwarf of G5004 as vase
G5055 Dwarf of G5005 as vase
G5056 Dwarf of G5006 as vase
G5057 Dwarf of G5007 as vase
G5058 Standing man with top hat "Mad Hatter" (1951)
G5059 Standing figurine with crown "King"
G5060 Female figurine with animal under her arm "Queen"
G5061 Standing rabbit with spectacles, heart on its chest
G5062 Standing girl with hands at her skirt "Alice"
G5063 Standing man with top hat and cigar "Walrus"
G5064 Standing man with paving stone on head "Carpenter"
G5065 Two men with caps standing side by side "Dee and Dum"
G5066 Standing bird with pipe "Dodo"
G5067 Standing man, playing card as body "Gardener Cards"
G5068 Wall-vase with deer Bambi and rabbit
G5069 "Queen" as rocking figurine
G5070 "King" as rocking figurine
G5071 Dressed bird with pipe as ashtray (1952)
G5072 Sitting elephant stretching up its trunk as ashtray

G5073 Standing duck as ice-hockey player on a round bowl
G5074 Small Duck as ice-hockey player on a round bowl
G5075 "Mickey Mouse" as hunter, beside stem, as vase
G5076 Running dog with artificial ears and tail
G5077 Kneeling Mickey Mouse going hunting
G5078 Mickey Mouse with book sitting on a stem
G5079 Sitting dog "instructions for hunting"
G5080 Round bowl with lips at rim, as ashtray
G5080A Not on list, but apparently a Dumbo ashtray
G5081 Standing mouse with left hand raised
G5082 Standing mouse with hands on belly "Father"
G5083 Standing mouse with left hand at ear "Mother"
G5084 Sitting cat with flower on its head
G5085 Laughing cat lying on its back with its forelegs
       crossed on its chest
G5086 Sitting elephant with large ears and vessel on back
G5087 Dressed rabbit lying flat on face with forelegs
       propped up
G5088 Standing man with top hat, hands on hips
G5089 Standing man with coffee pot in his hand
G5090 Standing man with cigar in right hand
G5091 Running rabbit with watch in hand
G5092 Sitting elephant with trunk raised as ashtray
G5093 Standing thick man as rocking figurine
G5094 Cinderella and Prince on round base
G5095 Cinderella on staircase with lost shoe
G5096 Cinderella with groom
G5097 Standing thick man with stick and cigar as rocking
       figurine
G5098A Sitting cat with head raised
G5098B Sitting cat with head turned to left
G5099 Sitting boy with plumed hat
G5100 Running boy with plumed hat and apple in hand
G5101 Dressed elephant and small rabbit
G5102 Dressed fox with top hat and walking stick
G5103 Dressed cat with top hat and walking stick
G5104 Round weaved small basket with a cat on its cover
G5105 Cat standing on bowl with wavy rim
G5106 Figurine of G5068 as ashtray with two lips
G5107 Figurine of G5065 as ashtray with two lips
G5108 Figurine of G5066 as ashtray with two lips
G5109 Rabbit of G5039 without vase
G5110 Standing thick man with cigar as liquor bottle
G5111 Bambi and frog on an oval base
G5112 Bambi of G5111 without base
G5113 Standing Bambi and sitting rabbit
G5114 Standing Bambi and sitting skunk
G5115 Bambi of G5114 without base
G5116 Bambi of G5022 without base
G5117 Standing Bambi with butterfly on tail
G5118 Sitting duck opening bill
G5119 Two kissing skunks
G5120 Two sitting rabbits on oval base
G5121 Standing owl spreading wings
G5122 Elephant of G5080A as single figurine
G5123 Duck of G5073 as single figurine
G5124 Duck of G5074 as single figurine
G5125 Cat with large ball
G5126 Duck of G5015 as single figurine
G5127 Duck of G5046 as single figurine
G5128 Sitting and lying rabbit without base
G5129 Frog of G5111 as single figurine
G5130 Skunk of G5114 as single figurine
G5131 Rabbit of G5113 as single figurine
G5132 Open book with standing figurine as display plaque
G5133 Open book with standing boy as display plaque
G5134 Standing bearded man with apron as liquor bottle
G5135 Cat with upright tail "Lucifer"
G5136 Rabbit of G5050 without holes
G5137 Rabbit of G5034 without holes
G5138 Cat Box of G5104 with holes
G5139 Bambi of G5117 with artificial butterfly
G5140 Lying deer and Bambi
G5141 Sitting dog "Bruno"
G5142 Standing duck with a hole in its bill for an artificial fly
G5143A Dressed pig with violin

G5143B Dressed pig with flute
G5143C Dressed pig with mouth-organ
G5144 Standing bird with scarf
G5145A Rabbit of G5120 as single figurine
G5145B Rabbit of G5120 as single figurine
G5146 Bambi of G5021 as ashtray with lip
G5147 Bambi of G5012 as ashtray with lip
G5148 Dwarf of G5005 as ashtray with lip
G5149 Sitting dog "Pluto" as perfume spender
G5150 Standing Bambi as perfume spender (1953)
G5151 Rabbit standing on its hind legs as perfume spender
G5152 Open book with Mickey Mouse as display plaque
G5153 Standing boy, hands on hips "Peter Pan"
G5154 Standing boy with teddy, "Peter Pan" and Michael
G5155 Kneeling water sprite on a round base "Mermaid"
G5156 Standing girl with wings "Tinker Bell"
G5157 Sitting boy "Peter Pan"
G5158 Standing figurine with a club in his left hand "Cubby"
G5159 Standing figurine made up as a fox "Foxy"
G5160 Cat of G5105 as ashtray with lip
G5161 Dog of G5149 as lamp stand (1954)
G5162 Ashtray G5148 without lip
G5163 Bambi of G5022 beside oval bowl
G5164 Boy of G5100 beside an oval bowl
G5165A Standing duck with butterfly on its tail as music box
G5165B Standing duck with butterfly on its bill as single figurine
G5166 Pig of G5143 beside a round bowl
G5167 Sitting dog "Susi" (1955) Lady
G5168 Sitting dog with its foreleg raised "Strolch" (Tramp)
G5169 Sitting bloodhound (Trusty)
G5170 Sitting terrier "York" (Jock)
G5171 Sitting dachshund "Dachsie"
G5172 "Bulldogge"
G5173 Pekinese "Peg"
G5174 Sitting cat "Si"
G5175 Sitting greyhound "Boris"
G5176 Sitting dog "Toughy"
G5177A Boy with rifle, bookend
G5177B Bear standing on hind legs, bookend
G5178 Drinking cup with handle and a kneeling boy in relief
G5179 Bowl with two jumping bears in relief
G5180A Standing boy with rifle, salt shaker
G5180B Standing bear, pepper shaker
G5181 Standing Bambi as perfume spender (1956)
G5182 "Susi" (Lady) with two brown dogs at one chain
G5183 "Strolch" (Tramp) with two dogs at one chain
G5184 "Susi" (Lady) and "Strolch" (Tramp) as group of dogs
G5186 Bambi of G5112 beside stump as lampstand (1957)
G5187 Bambi of B5139 beside stem as lampstand
G5188 Standing figurine with wings "Tinker Bell" (1959)
G5189 Kneeling figurine with wings "Tinker Bell"
G5190 Group of dogs with chain
G5191 Group of dogs with chain
G5192B Standing dog
G5193 2 Bambis of G5111 as a group without base (1960)
G5194 Bambis of G5116 and G5021 as a group without base
G5195 Bambis of G5111 and G5116 on base
G5197 Sitting Dalmatian (1961)
G5198 Lying Dalmatian
G5199 Sitting Dalmatian holding a heart in its muzzle
G5200 Barking small Dalmatian
G5201 Sitting small Dalmatian with a bone in its muzzle
G5202 Wall lamp "Donald Duck" in the vessel (1962)
G5203 Wall lamp "Donald Duck" with a ball in his hands
G5204 Basket Amendment Set rabbit of G5040 as salt
       and pepper shaker in a basket
G5205 Group of dogs with chain (1962)
G5206 Sitting bear with a little boy on its belly (1965)
G5300 Snow White plate (see P3690)
G5301 Mickey or Bambi theme park designs
G5310 Reissue of G5001-7, plus G5012 and new Prince
       figure, set 100 - 200
G5330 New design approach, 10 figures, Mickey or Minnie
       jogging; Mickey Tennis, stamp collecting or in
       garden; Donald fishing, playing video game or
       boating; or Minnie embroidering or working out.

These figures are being retailed for 25, 30 and 40 each.
G5340 Snow White (5-3/4") and Dwarfs (2-3/4"), set retail price 110.

G6000 GOOD HOUSEKEEPING CHILDREN'S PAGES

The April 1934 issue of *Good Housekeeping* magazine introduced four new features as part of a general revamping of the publication. One was a series by Walt Disney (see cover promotion poster for Apr '34 issue). There were 125 installments ending with the Sept '44 issue. None appeared in the Aug '39 number. All were single pages except Snow White (Nov and Dec '37) serialized in multi-pages over two issues, Pinocchio complete in two multi-page (Oct and Nov '39) and Bambi that ran as three single pages Sept to Nov '42. Four color pages ended Dec '41. The last 12 ran a Mother Goose Tale. The Studio treated these as an advance publicity outlet for upcoming releases so the run provides an interesting history of studio activities and character development during this period. Color pages 1 - 4 each. Feature movie sections 1 - 10 each. Two color pages 1 - 6 each.

G6000

G9105

G9250

G9111

80

G8900 GUM BALL/CANDY MACHINE

Such a vending machine was made by Hamilton Enterprises, Inc. (Kansas City, MO) 1938-41. Valued at 75 - 325. Pulver used a Borgfeldt wood Mickey figure in one of their red character models. Probably not authorized. Circa 1932-33. Value 100 - 600.

G9100 GUM CARDS, GUM WRAPPERS AND TRADING CARDS

Gum, Inc. issued Mickey Mouse bubble gum and cards in 1933. The first series of 48 cards could be mounted into a special album. There was a separate album for the second series of cards numbered 49-96. Mickey Mouse with the Movie Stars are numbered 97-120. No album is known. There was a different wrapper for the third series. Topps issued two Davy Crockett card series (1955-56) and a Zorro set (1958-59). Donruss did a special series for Disneyland's 10th aniversary in 1965. Treat Hobby Products printed collector cards in 1983. The British Anglo Confectionery set and Mickey's Sweet Cigarettes (Barratt and Co. Ltd.) are two of the more outstanding sets from London that were distributed in Canada. Various wrappers were made for gum products without cards.

G9103	Mickey Mouse (Gum, Inc)	1-48, each	1 - 5
G9104	Mickey Mouse (Gum, Inc)	49-96, each	2 - 6
G9105	Wrapper for G9103 and G9104		45 - 125
G9106	Mickey Mouse/Movie Stars (Gum, Inc.) 97-120, each		10 - 45
G9107	Wrapper for G9106		125 - 250
G9110	Snow White stick gum wrapper (Dietz)		1 - 10
G9111	Dopey bubble gum wrapper (Yankee Doodle)		8 - 50
G9115	Pinocchio stick gum wrapper (Dietz)		1 - 10
G9116	Jiminy Cricket bubble gum wrapper (Yankee Doodle)		8 - 50
G9200	Davy Crockett (80-orange backs) Topps, each		1 - 3
G9201	Davy Crockett (80-green backs) Topps, each		2 - 5
G9210	Zorro (88) Topps, each		1 - 3
G9220	Disneyland (66) Donruss, each		1 - 2
G9238	The Black Hole (88 - 21 stickers) Topps, set		3 - 10
G9240	TRON (66 cards - 8 stickers) 1981, set		3 - 10
G9250	Collector sets (5)- Mickey, Donald, Goofy, Snow White and Bambi (Treat Hobby), each set		1 - 3

Licensed manufacturers — Dietz Gum Company (Chicago) 1933-41; The Donruss Co. (Memphis, TN) 1965 and 1981; Glenn Confections, Inc. (Buffalo, NY) 1937-39; Gum, Inc. (Philadelphia, PA) 1933-37; Topps Chewing Gum, Inc. (Brooklyn, NY) 1955-56, 58-59 and 79; Treat Hobby Products, Inc. (Fullerton, CA) 1983 and Yankee Doodle Gum Co. (Chicago) 1938-41.

Also see — BREAD CARDS AND PREMIUMS; CANDY, CANDY BOXES AND WRAPPERS; and GAMES — CARD.

G9700 GUNS, SWORDS AND OTHER PLAY WEAPONS

Play weapons first appeared in the TV Mickey Mouse Club play sets. Davy Crockett and Zorro (see Z5000) were the major source of weapon merchandise, but animated features produced swords and a dueling magic wand.

G9720	Mickey Mouse Explorers or Western Club outfit gun, holster and accessories (Daisy), each	12 - 55
G9750	Davy Crockett pistol and holster set (Daisy)	6 - 40
G9751	Davy Crockett pistol or pop gun (Daisy), each	5 - 35
G9752	Davy Crockett powder horn (Daisy)	5 - 20
G9760	Prince Phillip's Sword (Empire)	4 - 25
G9763	Sword in the Stone (Empire)	4 - 25
G9764	Merlin's Magic Wand (GE)	4 - 30

Licensed manufacturers — Daisy Manufacturing Co. (Plymouth, MI) 1955-59; L. M. Eddy Mfg. Co., Inc. (NYC) 1955-57; Empire Plastics, Inc. (NYC) 1959-63 and General Electric Wiring Service Dept. (Providence, RI) 1963-64.

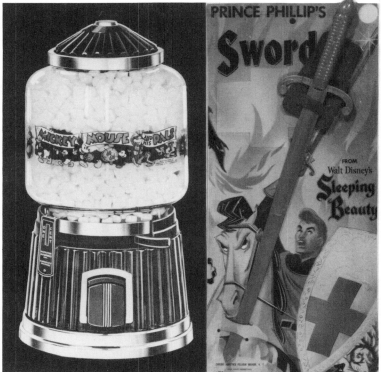

G8900   G9760

G9720

G9220

G9752

81

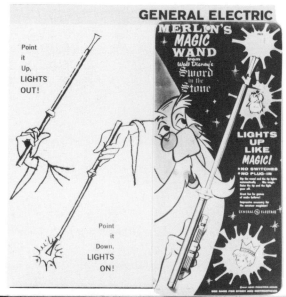

G9764

PLAY SWORD

Plastic sword with simulated jewels on hilt, blue blade and green scabbard, mounted on colorful shield-like display card. Sword is 25 inches long, and 31 inches in scabbard.

$1 Suggested retail

FOR ALL INFORMATION
CONTACT:

Empire Plastics, Inc.
200 Fifth Avenue
New York, N. Y.

G9763

H1001-H1013

H1003

H1046

H1075-H1085

H1020   H1019

H1030-H1038

H1040-H1051

H1065   H1066

H1000 HAGEN-RENAKER CERAMICS

Hagen-Renaker (Monrovia, CA) famous for miniature ceramic Disney figures, was licensed through a sales representative firm, George Good Co. (LA) from 1955-61. *Lady and the Tramp* figures were sold exclusively at Disneyland the first year. In 1956 the company added figures from *Alice in Wonderland, Bambi, Cinderella, Dumbo,* and *Mickey Mouse Club* cartoon characters. Larger figures were distributed nationally under the Designer's Workshop name: Snow White, the Seven Dwarfs, Jiminy Cricket and other characters. Banks and cookie jars were 1956 DW products. Miniatures were soon included. The *Peter Pan* and *Fantasia* figures were added in 1957; *Snow White and 7 Dwarf miniatures* in 1958; and *Sleeping Beauty* characters in 1959. Banks and cookie jars were made for H-R by other potteries. A larger set of Hagen-Renaker *Fantasia* figures were produced for sale at theme park Disneyana shops in the '80's. Additional figures for this series and a Country Bear Jamboree set were planned, but not produced. Stan Pawlowski provided information and photos from his collection for this Hagen-Renaker section.

H1055-H1063

H1015   H1016

H1001	Lady (sold later as "non-Disney"), orig.	10 - 50
H1002	Tramp	20 - 100
H1003	Scamp, Ruffles or Fluffy, each	5 - 25
H1006	Scooter, Jock or Trusty, each	10 - 50
H1009	Si or Am, each	10 - 50
H1011	Pedro or Dachsie, each	10 - 70
H1013	Peg or Bull, each	20 - 100
H1015	Alice	20 - 100
H1016	Mad Hatter, March Hare or Caterpillar, each	15 - 75
H1019	Cinderella	10 - 110
H1020	Gus or Jaq, each	10 - 75
H1022	Bambi or Faline, each	20 - 130
H1024	Flower or Thumper, each	15 - 70
H1026	Dumbo or Timothy Mouse, each	15 - 70
H1030	Mickey as band leader	20 - 110
H1031	Pluto or Goofy	20 - 120
H1033	Donald Duck	20 - 100
H1034	Scrooge McDuck	15 - 85
H1035	Huey, Louie or Dewey, playing baseball, each	10 - 70
H1038	Chip or Dale, each	10 - 70
H1040	Peter Pan	20 - 110
H1041	Wendy, John or Michael, each	20 - 100
H1044	Michael's Teddy Bear or Nana	10 - 60
H1046	Tinker Bell — flying	20 - 110
H1047	Tinker Bell — kneeling	20 - 100
H1048	Tinker Bell — shelf sitter	20 - 130
H1049	Reclining Mermaid, blonde or redhead, each	10 - 50
H1051	Kneeling Mermaid, blonde or redhead, each	10 - 50
H1055	Bacchus	15 - 85
H1056	Faun #1, #2 or #3, each	10 - 50
H1059	Unicorn	15 - 95
H1060	Baby Unicorn or Baby Pegasus, each	10 - 60
H1063	Greek Column	3 - 15
H1065	Snow White	15 - 85
H1066	Seven Dwarfs, set	50 - 160
H1075	Sleeping Beauty	20 - 100
H1076	Prince Phillip	20 - 100
H1077	Maleficent and Raven	100 - 475
H1078	Flora, Fauna, or Merryweather, each	10 - 60
H1081	King Stefan or King Hubert, each	15 - 85
H1083	The Queen	10 - 65
H1084	Samson	50 - 300
H1085	Rabbit, Squirrel, Owl, Cardinal or Bluebird, each	10 - 40

Larger (about 3″ to 4 1/2″) Designer's Workshop Figures

H1090	Bambi or Flower, each	20 - 100
H1091	Jiminy Cricket or Figaro, each	15 - 85
H1092	Snow White or Dumbo, each	15 - 95
H1093	Seven Dwarfs, each	10 - 20
H1100	Practical Pig, Thumper, Dumbo or Figaro cookie jar, each	20 - 150
H1103	Practical Pig, Thumper, Dumbo, Figaro or Lady bank, each	15 - 140
H1120	Mickey as the Sorcerer's Apprentice	20 - 40
H1121	Broom with water bucket	10 - 20
H1122	Bacchus	15 - 30
H1123	Baby Pegasus, pink, blue or black, each	10 - 20

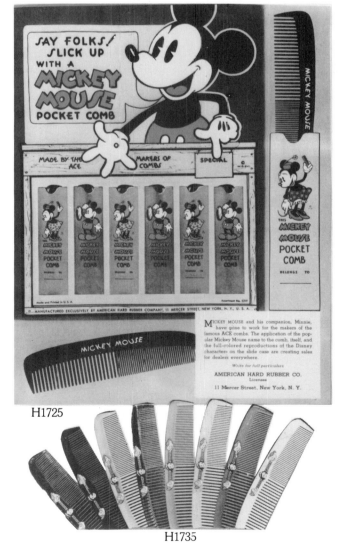

H1725

H1735

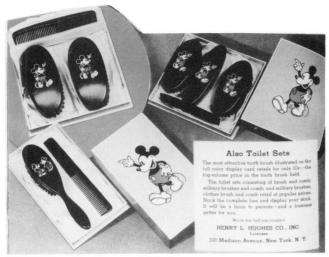

H1720

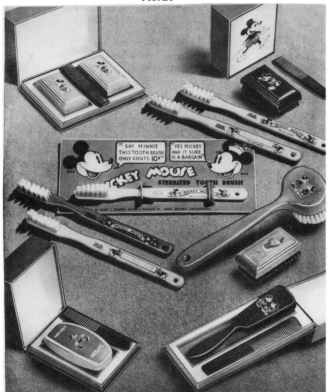

H1732

H2140

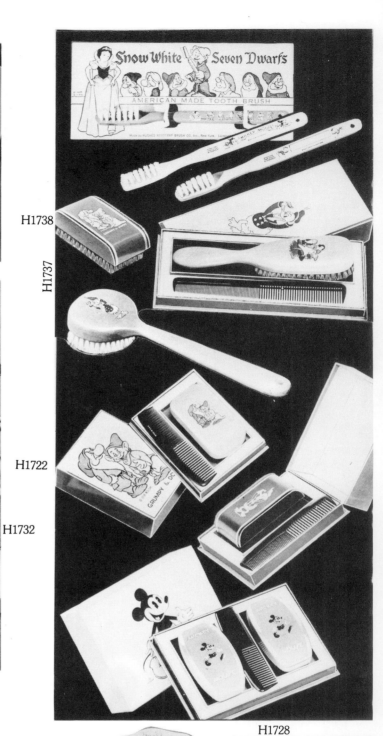

H1738

H1737

H1722

H1728

H1765   H1766

H2120

84

| H1126 Ostrich | 25 - 45 |
| H1127 Mushroom | 2 - 4 |

H1700 HAIR BRUSHES, COMBS AND ACCESSORIES

Hair care products were among the earliest licensed. Cohn and Rosenburger had Mickey and Three Pigs comb case sets. The 1934 merchandise catalog listed Henry L. Hughes, an early brush licensee. Disney characters have appeared on grooming sets or individual brushes and combs almost continuously ever since.

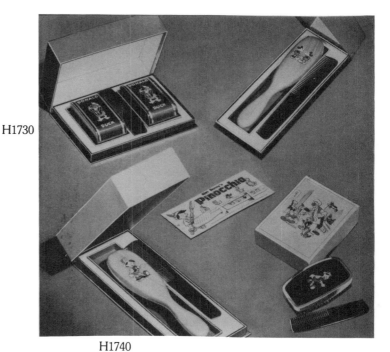

H1730

H1710	Cohn & Rosenberger, enameled comb and case	15 - 65
H1720	Hughes black wood handle brush sets	10 - 50
H1721	Individual brushes from H1720 (1934-35), each	4 - 15
H1722	Mickey/Minnie clothes brush (Hughes)	5 - 20
H1725	Pocket comb in Mickey or Minnie case (American)	5 - 35
H1728	Mickey hair brush set, aluminum clad handles (Hughes)	8 - 40
H1729	Individual brushes from H1728 (1936-37), each	4 - 13
H1730	Same as H1728, but Donald Duck	9 - 45
H1731	Individual brushes from H1730, each	5 - 18
H1732	Donald Duck hair brush (Hughes)	5 - 20
H1735	Snow White comb (Lapin-Kurley)	3 - 12
H1737	Snow White hair brush and comb (Hughes)	4 - 18
H1738	Grumpy/Dopey boys hairbrush and comb (Hughes)	3 - 15
H1740	Pinocchio hair brush and comb (Hughes)	4 - 18
H1741	Pinocchio clothes brush	4 - 18
H1760	Snow White 3 piece translucent plastic dresser set (George)	5 - 23
H1764	Mickey or Donald, Sterling comb and brush set (American Metalcraft), each	10 - 50
H1765	Mickey or Donald comb and mirror set (Loma), each	3 - 15
H1766	Mickey or Donald figural handle brushes (Loma), each	2 - 12

Licensed manufacturers — American Hard Rubber Co. (NYC) 1935-37, combs; American Metalcraft Company (Attleburo, MA) 1947-48, Aristocrat Leather Products, Inc. (NYC) 1955-63; Herbert George Co. (Chicago) 1946-48; Henry L. Hughes Co., Inc. (NYC) 1934-37, succeeded by Hughes-Autograf Brush Co., Inc. (NYC) 1938-41; Lapin Kurley Kew. Inc. (NYC) 1938-40; Loma Plastics, Inc. (Ft. Worth, TX) 1948-53 and Stance Industries (Hawppauge, NY) 1982-84.

H2100 HANDKERCHIEFS AND HANKY BOOKS

Waldburger, Tanner & Co. (St. Gall, Switzerland) was awarded the first official Disney license aggreement on March 27, 1930 to make handkerchiefs. Several licensees combined to provide Disney hankies continuously to 1965 — and in a number of years since. Herrmann was the largest producer of embroidered and print hankies. They were sold in illustrated boxes and "Hankeyventure" books. The books had slits into which the folded hankies were placed.

| H2101 | Waldburger, Tanner & Co, designs, each | 10 - 50 |
| H2110 | Voly & Fawcett Mickey Mouse, each | 3 - 15 |

The Herrmann Handkerchief Co., Inc. H2120-H2175

H2120	Embroidered set of 3 in box	8 - 35
H2121	Embroidered set of 7 in box	20 - 100
H2122	Individual designs from H2120-H2121, each	2 - 10
H2123	Silly Symphony embroidered set in box	15 - 65
H2124	Individual designs from H2123, each	3 - 15
H2128	Print Mickey or Silly Symphony sets in box (30's)	10 - 45
H2129	Individual designs from H2128, each	2 - 12
H2130	Mickey, Mickey/Minnie or Mickey/Pluto Hankerchief purse, each	5 - 30
H2135	Snow White & 7 Dwarfs set of 8	20 - 100
H2136	Snow White & 7 Dwarfs set of 3	7 - 28
H2137	Individual designs from H2135 or H2136, each	2 - 12
H2138	Snow White & 7 Dwarfs, print sets, each	7 - 80
H2139	Individual print designs from H2138, each	2 - 10
H2140	Hankyventures book with 8 hankies (1940)	25 - 100
H2141	Print hankies from H2140, each	1 - 5
H2142	Mickey and gang, embroidered, boxed set of 8 (1940)	25 - 100
H2143	Mickey and gang, embroidered, boxed set of 3	8 - 35
H2144	Individual designs from H2142 or H2143, each	1 - 5

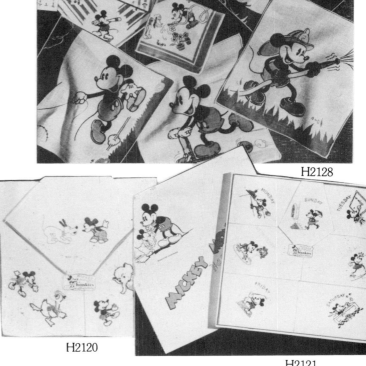

H1740

H2128

H2120

H2121

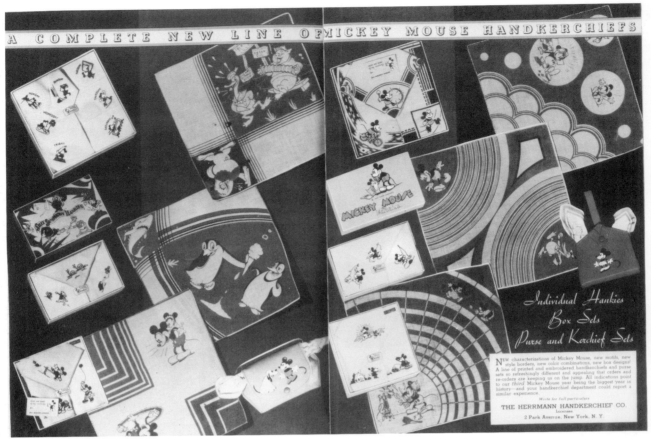

H2128

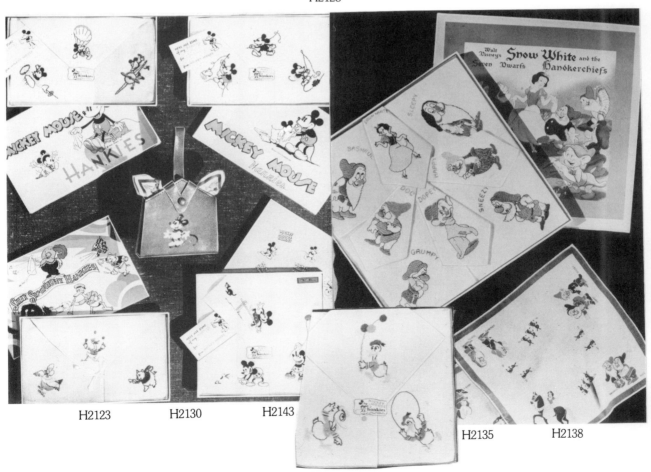

H2123   H2130   H2143   H2135   H2138

H2150	Pinocchio, embroidered, boxed set of 6 (1940)	20 - 80
H2151	Pinocchio, embroidered, boxed set of 3	8 - 30
H2152	Individual designs from H2150 or H2151, each	1 - 5
H2153	Pinocchio, print, boxed sets, each	8 - 35
H2154	Individual designs from H2153, each	1 - 5
H2158	Bambi hanky book	8 - 60
H2170	Mid-40's Mickey, boxed sets, each	5 - 25
H2175	Individual print designs from H2170, each	1 - 4
H2190	Snow White & 7 Dwarfs, set of 8 (Wolf) 1938	25 - 100
H2191	Mickey, friends and Silly Symphony, set of 10 (Wolf) 1938	35 - 120
H2192	Individual designs from H2190 or H2191, each	2 - 12
H2193	Print Snow White & 7 Dwarfs, set of 4 (Wolf)	8 - 18
H2194	Individual designs from H2193	1 - 3
H2200	Rain's boxed sets of 3, 4 different, each	5 - 25
H2201	Individual designs from H2200, each	1 - 4

Licensed manufacturers — The Herrmann Handkerchief Co., Inc. (NYC) 1932-51; Saul S. Negreann, Inc. (NYC) 1975-76; S. E. Rains Co., Ltd. (NYC) 1948-65; Max Simon & Associates (LA) 1968; Voly & Fawcett (NYC) 1931-32; Waldburger, Tanner & Co. (St. Gall, Switzerland) via Waldburger & Huber (NYC) 1930 and Bernhard Wolf (NYC) 1938-39.

H3000 HATS AND CAPS

Hats and caps come in several categories — Mickey endorsed dress variety with inside markings only, sports models with external markings, novelty and character hats and special hats such as a Davy Crockett coonskin hat or rubber swim caps. None are very valuable or sought after. Values range up to 25 - 30 for an early high class model. Sports or knit hats go for up to 10 - 15 with the more interesting novelty hats in the same range. See M5000 for Mickey Mouse Ears.

Licensed manufacturers — George S. Bailey Hat Co., Inc. (LA) 1955-58; Bamberger-Reinthal Co. (Cleveland, OH) 1972+; Benay Albee Novelty Co. (Maspeth, NY) 1956, 59, 68-84; Cal-Fame Hat Co. (LA) 1945-48; California Headwear Inc. (LA) 1982-83; The Cudahy Packaging Co. (Pinocchio hat premiums for Sunlight Butter) 1940-41; Elrene Mfg. Corp. (NYC) 1952-53; B. J. Goldenberg, Inc. (NYC) 1943, ladies' millinery; Josie Accessories, Inc. (NYC) 1952-55; Ira G. Katz (NYC) 1938-39; L. Lewis & Son (NYC) 1939-41; Newark Felt Novelty (Newark, NJ) 1939-41; Philbert Hat (NYC) 1939-41; Reliable Knitting Works (Milwaukee, WI) 1946-49, 55-57, 77-84; The Rockmore Company, Inc. (NYC) 1949-50; Stadium Sports-Headwear Co. (NYC) 1939-40; Charles Tobias Bro. & Co. (Cincinnati, OH) 1933-40; Weathermac Corp. (NYC) 1955-56 and Welded Plastics Corp. (NYC) 1955-56.

H3000

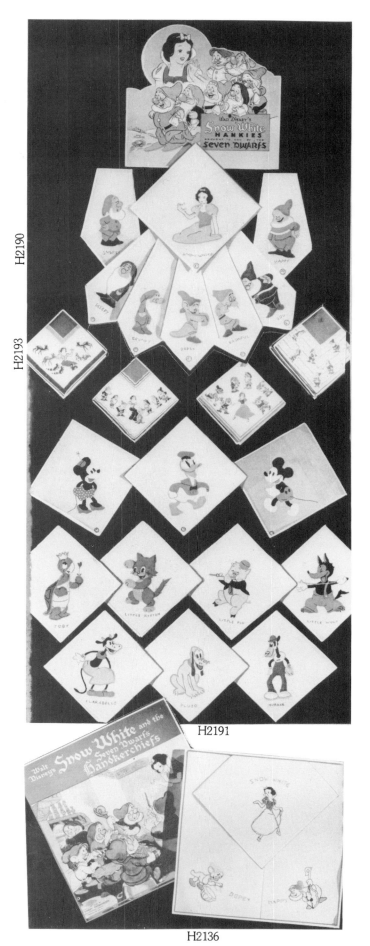

H2190

H2193

H2191

H2136

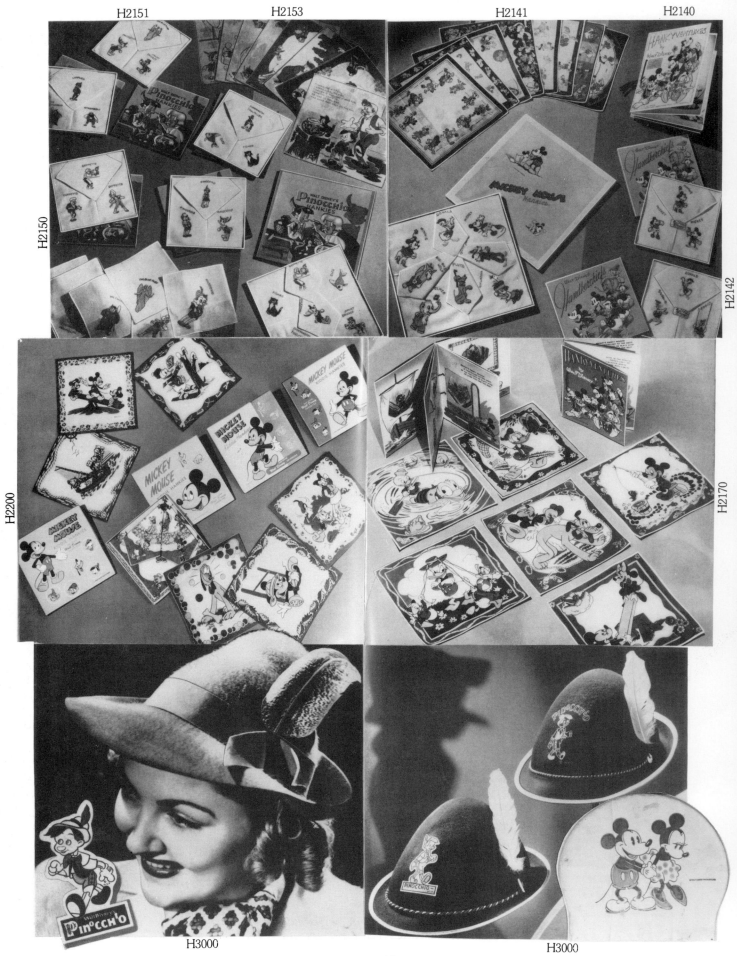

H2151 H2153 H2141 H2140

H2150

H2142

H2200

H2170

H3000

H3000

88

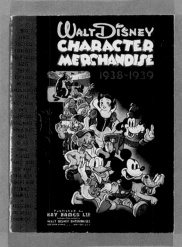

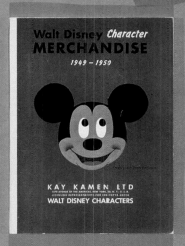

H6000 HOUSEHOLD GOODS; PRODUCTS AND MISC.

This is a catch-all category for personal and household products not elsewhere classified. If it is an oddball piece, this is a good place to start the search. Values range from .50 to maybe 15 or 20 tops for older pieces.

Licensed manufacturers — Amcor Group, Ltd. (NYC) 1982-83, hand showers and shower heads; Black Leaf Products (Elgin, IL) 1972-80, outdoor fun shower; Dapol Plastics (Worcester, MA) 1971-72, lawn decorations; J. H. Erbrich Products Co. (Indianapolis, IN) 1948-50, Snow White Ammonia & Bleach; F & M Shoe Shine Kits (Hollywood, CA) 1954-55; James Feldman (Brooklyn, NY) 1939-41, washing compound; JFD Electronics (Oxford, NC) 1975-77, indoor TV antennas; Nitec Paper Corp. (Niagara Falls, NY) 1980-81, facial tissues; Pacific Waxed Paper (Seattle, WA) 1940-41; Plascor Inc. (See Dapol Plastics); Plastic Metal Mfg. Co. (Chicago) 1957-62, plastic containers, Freez ur pops, etc; Private Label Dental Floss, Inc. (Verona, NJ) 1982-83, dental floss and related products; K. J. Quinn & Co. Inc. (Malden, MA) 1953 and 1955; Scuffy shoe polish; Rayette, Inc. (St. Paul, MN) 1953, shampoo; Sharp and Dohme (Sucrets related advertising) 1947-48; Foster D. Snell Sales Corp. (NYC and Rochester, NY) 1931-32, cigarette snappers and door stops; Stonite Company, Inc. (NYC) 1930-32, Mickey door stops and cigarette snuffers; Tiger Home Products, Inc. (Princeton, NJ) 1979-81, wall hooks; Topco Toys, Inc. (NYC) 1982, soap-sponge and holder, toothpaste dispenser, and vinyl doorknob covers; Triangle Paper Bag Manufacturing Co. (Covington, KY) 1958-59, paper shopping bags; Union Carbide Corp. (Danbury, CT) 1984, Glad sandwich bags; U. S. Plywood Corporation (NYC) 1970-71, glues and adhesives; Wilton Enterprises, Inc. (Chicago) 1972-84, cake pan kits, sugar molds and plastic mold kits; and Woodlets, Inc. (Buffalo, NY) 1982, TRON air freshener supplied by Scent-Pak, Inc. (Baltimore, MD).

I1500 ICE CREAM AND RELATED PRODUCTS

Kay Kamen's Mickey Mouse Ice Cream Cone promotion in 1933 began a relationship that continues to date. The ice cream is gone, but posters, bags, Kay Kamen cone dollars, cartons, etc. remain to document these products for collectors. There were a number of ice cream premiums listed at ADVERTISING DISPLAYS, BOOKS, and GAMES — CARD. Values are .50 - 25 for older advertising items.

Licensed manufacturers — Clarson Dairy Co. (Richland Center, WI) 1953; Gold Bond Ice Cream Co. (Green Bay, WI) 1975-84, Mouseketeer Bars, frozen ice sticks and snow cones; Ice Cream Novelties, Inc.(NYC) 1948-53, bags and wrappers; Milko Cone and Baking Co., Inc. (NYC) 1938-41; Northern Dairy Co. (Marquette, MI) 1953; Northwest Cone Co., Inc. (Chicago) 1941-43; J. D. Roszell Co. (Peoria, IL) 1939-40, ice cream cups; Southern Dairies, Inc. (Washington, DC) 1936-40; and Vroman-Shaver Ice Cream Co. (Toledo, OH) 1953.

I2000 ICE SHOWS

Ice Capades of 1949 (beginning fall of 1948) introduced Disney characters in the lavish costume ice show tradition. Snow White and the Seven Dwarfs were featured. The 1950 edition featured Mickey, Minnie, Donald, Pinocchio and Dumbo. Cinderella followed in 1952. There have been four modern Disney Ice Shows produced in conjunction with Irvin Feld and Kenneth Feld — Walt Disney Productions World on Ice, Walt Disney's Great Ice Odyssey, Walt Disney's World on Ice, and Walt Disney's Magic Kingdom on Ice. Souvenirs from these shows are valued at 2 - 12.

I1500   H3000

H6000

I2000

I2000

I2000   I5000

VANGUARD CORPORATION
CHICOPEE, MASS.

0223-9004 Asst.

Contains:
Mickey — 6 ea.   Dumbo — 6 ea.
Donald — 6 ea.   Pluto — 6 ea.
0223-9005 Mickey 24 ea.
Character inflatables are poly bagged with metal grommet.
approx. 24" tall.

0223-9005

0223-9100

Inflatable Toys
0223-9100 Asst.
Contains:
Mickey — 10 ea.   Dumbo — 4 ea.
Donald — 6 ea.   Dalmatian — 4 ea.
Character inflatables are poly bagged with metal grommet.
Approx. 12" tall.

I5000

IDEAL TOY CORPORATION
200 Fifth Avenue, New York, N. Y. 10010   Contact: Abe Kent

VINYL INFLATABLES

Eeyore   Pooh   Piglet   Tigger   Kanga and Roo

C-5623-4 — 6 piece assortment. 80¢ each

Eeyore

A-5624-2
2 Winnie the Pooh styles. $1.00 each

B-5625-9
$1.00 each

Tigger   Piglet   Kanga and Roo

I5000

DOUGHBOY INDUSTRIES, INC.
PLASTICS DIVISION
NEW RICHMOND, WIS.

HUFF·N·PUFFS

FLOWER

$1.50

I5000

MICKEY MOUSE KIDDIE JEWELRY

NECKLACES
with Personality. Mickey and Minnie in bright colored enamel

BRACELETS
Bangle and Dangle engraved with likenesses of the two film favorites, Mickey and Minnie Mouse.

SILVER BELT BUCKLES

RINGS

Mickey Mouse Kiddie Jewelry for the thousands of children who love Mickey and Minnie. Here is one of the most extensive and beautiful lines of kiddie jewelry ever produced.

Newspaper Advertising

Arrangement of co-operative newspaper advertising with local retailers when Mickey Mouse is in town will pay dividends to the theatre and to the local stores.

Window Displays

There is a great active market waiting to be sold. Put Punch in your campaign. Window displays featuring Mickey Mouse Kiddie Jewelry will ring up new records on the cash register!

LAPEL BUTTONS AND BROOCHES
for Mickey Mouse Club Members

BIB HOLDERS

MESH BAGS
Enamelled mesh bags decorated with charming Mickey Mouse figure.

COHN & ROSENBERGER, Inc.

47 West 34th Street
New York City

110 Wellington Street West
Toronto, Ontario

I6065

J2000

I5000 INFLATABLES

Inflatable figures, beach balls and pool toys have been around since Seiberling's initial Mickey and Pluto in 1934. Donald and the Big Bad Wolf were added in 1935. There have been a number of licensees since, but as mentioned earlier, latex rubber used for early figures rots under normal circumstances. Vinyl may fare better, but inflatables hold little collecting interest because of their self-destructing nature. Rare is one that brings more than a few dollars.

Licensed manufacturers — Buzza-Cardozo (Anaheim, CA) 1970-71; Dough-boy Industries, Inc. (New Richmond, WI) 1948-49; Haugh's Products Ltd. (Canadian) 1949-50; Ideal Toy Corp. (Hollis, NY) 1968-82; Kestral Corp. (Springfield, MA) 1953-54; W. S. Rainford Products, Inc. (Closter, NJ) 1947-48; Seiberling Latex Products Co. (Akron, OH) 1934-42; Vanguard Corp. (Chicopee, MA) 1949-53; Walt Disney Distributing Co. (Lake Buena Vista, FL) 1971-77; and Zee Toys, Inc. (Long Beach, CA) 1983-84.

I6000 IRON-ON APPLIQUÉS AND TRANSFERS

Bondex (Industrial Tape) made a popular series of iron-on appliqués. There were penny and premium transfers of Mickey, also a large series of Disney designed military insignia transfers. There have probably been hundreds of T-shirt transfer designs, but generally these are applied to a shirt before sold. Many transfers also came with sewing patterns.

I6025	Bondex appliques (3-pack), each	2 - 10
I6040	Mickey with banjo	2 - 8
I6045	Military insignias (2 per sheet) each sheet	3 - 12
I6065	Happy Soup Club (Premium)	2 - 8

Licensed manufacturer — Industrial Tape Corp. (New Brunswick, NJ) 1944-50. Other licensees not known.

J1000 JACK-IN-THE-BOXES

Marks Brothers Co. (NYC) produced a Mickey version in 1936 followed by Dopey as a clown in 1939. Value 15 - 125 each. Spear Products Co. (NYC) did Donald and Mickey designs 1946-49 (wooden boxes) and was also licensed in 1958-61. Value 8 - 55. CBS Toys produced musical pop-up models 1979-84. Value 2 - 10.

J2000 JEWELRY (EXCEPT RINGS)

Character Jewelry has been produced in materials ranging from plastic to platinum set with diamonds. Cohn & Rosenburger produced some of the most collectible jewelry (1931-36). Brier Manufacturing runs a close second with collectors. Cartier was a jewelry licensee for early animated features and again since 1981. Others are listed below.

Cohn & Rosenberger, Inc. J2020-J2058

I5000

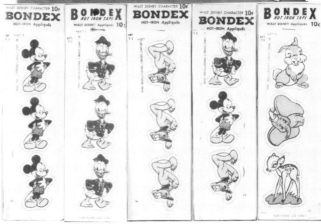

I6025

J2023   J2022

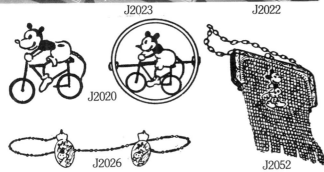

J2020   J2026   J2052

J2030-J2037

J2056   J2054

J2075-J2086

J2240

J2020	Mickey Lapel button or brooch (1931-32), each	10 - 100
J2022	Mickey necklace (1931-36)	9 - 90
J2023	Mickey bracelet, solid or chain (1931-36), each	9 - 90
J2025	Mickey silver belt buckle (1931-32)	6 - 60
J2026	Mickey bib holder (1931-32)	5 - 50
J2030	3 Pigs necklaces, 2 designs (1933), each	6 - 60
J2032	3 Pigs enameled bracelets, 3 designs, each	7 - 75
J2035	3 Pigs, wide band enameled bracelet	8 - 80
J2036	3 Pigs sweater enameled pin	6 - 60
J2037	3 Pigs pendant, 2 designs, each	6 - 60
J2040	Mickey enameled bracelets, 2 designs (1934), each	8 - 80
J2042	Mickey "jeweled" pendant	9 - 90
J2044	Minnie "jeweled" bracelet	9 - 90
J2045	Mickey or Minnie illustrated mesh purse, each	20 - 175
J2047	Mickey disc pendent	7 - 70
J2050	3 Pigs mesh coin purse	20 - 150
J2051	Mickey/Minnie mesh coin purse	20 - 175
J2052	Mickey mesh coin purse	20 - 200
J2053	3 Pigs enameled purse	20 - 175
J2054	Mickey/Minnie World's Fair, enameled purse	25 - 250
J2055	Mickey/Minnie/Pluto enameled purse	20 - 200
J2056	Mickey/Minnie enameled purse	20 - 200
J2058	3 Pigs match safe, green or orange, ea.	10 - 30
J2060	Mickey glass bubble tie bar	5 - 45

Brier Manufacturing Company J2075-J2140

J2075	Mickey or Minnie cloisonne pin, each	10 - 50
J2077	Donald or Pluto cloisonne pin, each	10 - 55
J2079	Mickey/Minnie, Mickey/Pluto or Mickey/ Donald sweater clasp, each	20 - 100
J2082	Pendant necklace- Mickey, Minnie, Donald or Pluto, each	10 - 50
J2086	Bracelet — same character choice as J2082, each	10 - 50
J2100	Snow White or Dwarf enameled pin, each	4 - 20
J2108	Snow White or Dwarf painted wood composition, each	5 - 30
J2116	Mickey wood composition pin, play violin, trumpet or drum, each	5 - 30
J2119	Donald wood composition pin, playing piccolo	5 - 30
J2120	Ferdinand the Bull wood composition pin	5 - 30
J2122	Pluto, giant wood composition pin	7 - 40
J2130	Pinocchio, Jiminy Cricket or Cleo plastic character pins, each	4 - 20
J2135	Same characters as J2130 as pendants, each	5 - 25
J2140	Pinocchio/Jiminy Cricket sweater clasp or bar pin, each	5 - 25
J2150	Cartier gold enameled character pins — Snow White, Dwarfs, Ferdinand, Pinocchio and others, each	25 - 200
J2165	Cartier character money clip	25 - 200
J2170	Ferdinand, rear view, against rhinestone fence	5 - 25
J2173	Authentics wood carved pieces, each	15 - 55
J2175	Speidel character disc bracelets, necklaces, bar	

J2100-J2119

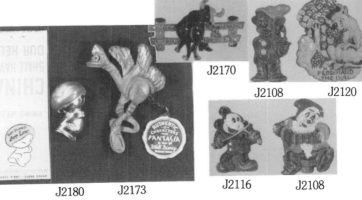

J2170

J2108   J2120

J2180   J2173

J2116   J2108

C6020

J2150   J2165

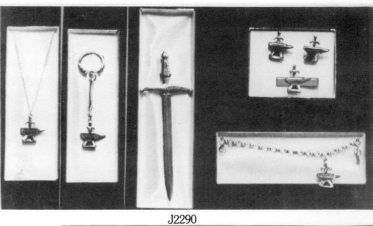

J2290

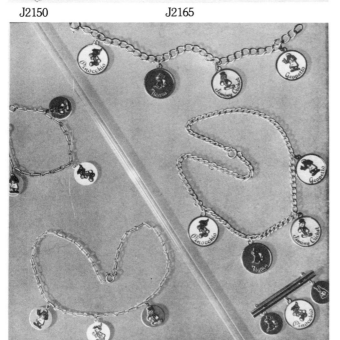

J2175

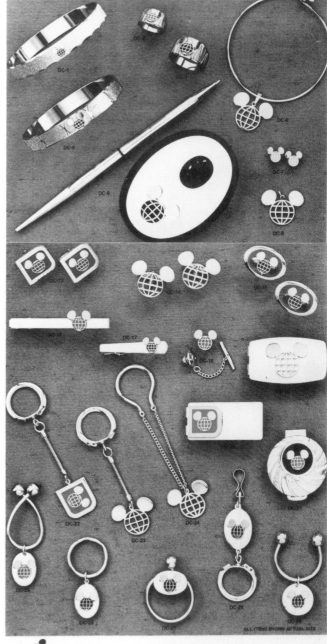

J2470

J2470

102

	pins, Pinocchio and probably Snow White, each	5 - 25	
J2180	Hop Low (China Relief)	8 - 40	
J2200	Alpha-Craft pins, each	6 - 32	
J2220	Charmore gold plated character pins — Mickey, Minnie, Donald, Pluto, Thumper, Practical Pig and others, each	6 - 32	
J2240	Eastern Jewelry character pins, plastic or metal. Heads moved on metal pins. Metal 7 - 40; plastic	4 - 20	
J2260	Dexter character pins; cufflinks; tie tack and bars; and necklaces — Mickey, Lady and the Tramp, Davy Crockett and Sword in the Stone, plus Snow White re-release, heavy non-precious metal. Range	1 - 15	
J2290	Sword in the Stone pins, bracelets, key ring & pendants (1963) Arden Range	1 - 10	
J2400	Theme park souvenir jewelry, 50's and 60's	1 - 25	
J2470	Theme park souvenir jewelry, post 70's	1 - 15	

Licensed manufacturers — Alpha-Craft (NYC) 1946-47; Arden Jewelry Mfg. Co. (Providence, RI) 1963; Authentics (NYC) 1941-1942; Beatrix Jewelry Co. (Pawtucket, RI) 1968; Arthur Beir & Co. Inc. (Providence, RI) 1935-42; Brier Mfg. Co. (Providence, RI) 1935-42, 1955; Cartier, Inc. (NYC) 1937-42, 81-84; The Charmore Company (NYC) 1946; Cohn & Rosenberger (NYC) 1931-36, 41-42; Floyd L. Cooper (Huntington Park, CA) 1933-34; Coro, Inc. (See Eastern Jewelry); Danal Jewelry Co. (Providence RI) 1970-71; Ms. Dee (Mound, MN) 1982; Delta Jewelry and Casting Co. (LA) 1945-48; Dexter Mfg. Co., Inc. (Providence, RI) 1953, 56, 68. 70-84; Eastern Jewelry Mfg., Inc. (NYC) 1948-53, 56; Howard Eldon Ltd. (Van Nuys, CA) 1972-84; F & V Mfg. Co., Inc. (E. Providence, RI) 1945-47; Flights of Fancy (Santa Monica, CA) 1982-83; Franklin Mint Corp. (Franklin Center, PA) 1982, 100th Anniversary Winnie the Pooh pendant; Hickok Belt Co. (Rochester, NY) 1970-71; Martime Jewelry Co. (NYC) 1970-71; Sloan & Co. (NYC) 1934-40; Speidel Co. (Providnce, RI) 1938-41; T. N. P. Jewels and Design Co. (NYC) 1977; Walt Disney Distributing Co. (Lake Buena Vista, FL) 1971-77; and E. K. Wertheimer and Son, Inc. (NYC) 1942-43, 60-61.

SPECIAL NOTICE — There are many jewelry pieces sold at Disney theme parks and elsewhere that look old, but are not. There are metal bracelets that resemble early Cohn & Rosenberger designs, an "antique jewelry" line depicting Steamboat Willie and pie-cut eyes Mickey and Minnie. None of these were sold for over 15. Most sell in the 2 - 7 price range.

K1000 KALEIDOSCOPES

Admiral Toy Co. (Chicago) made Mickey Mouse Club models. Steven Mfg. Co. (St. Louis) made Wonderful World of Color and Babes in Toyland kaleidoscopes 1961-63. Hallmark, Inc. (Kansas City, MO) produced a 40's looking one in 1978.

K1025	Admiral Toy Co. (1956-57)	3 - 15
K1030	Steven models	2 - 12
K1050	Hallmark	1 - 5

K2000 KEY CHAINS AND CASES

Cohn & Rosenberger made a key chain in the early 30's and many manufacturers have included them in their lines over the years. There have been hundreds of theme park metal and plastic key chains. Perhaps there is a collector out there who will sort it all out for us someday. Many are pictured here and in the jewelry classification. Few sell for more than a few dollars. Recent plastic key chains go for .25 - .50.

Licensed manufacturers — Aristocrat Leather Products, Inc. (NYC) 1955-63; Lido Toy Co. (NYC) 1954-55; Monogram Products, Inc. (Largo, FL) 1972-84 and most other jewelry and plastic products manufacturers.

Also see JEWELRY and PLASTIC TOYS AND NOVELTIES — MISCELLENEOUS

K3000 KITES

Marks Brothers Co. (NYC) made a Mickey paper kite throughout the 30's and a Dopey version in conjunction with Disney's first feature. Records do not show any 40's or 60's makers, but it is hard to imagine that someone didn't make them.

K3005	Marks Mickey or Dopey, each	5 - 45
K3060	Admiral Kite	3 - 20
K3070	Other makers	1 - 8

Licensed manufacturers- Admiral Toy Co. (Chicago) 1956-57; Hi-Flier Mfg. Co., Inc. (Decatur, IL) 1975-81 then as a Damon Co. (Penrose, CO) 1982-84; Marks Brothers Co. (Boston) 1934-41, 46-48; Renselaar Corp.

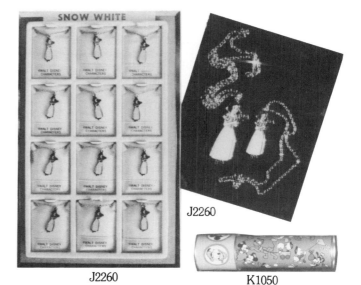

J2260

J2260

K1050

K2000

K3005

K2000

K3005

103

K5023

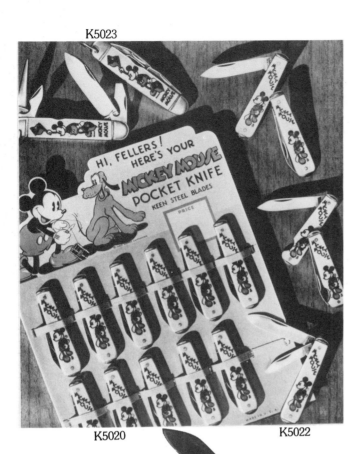

K5020

K5022

K5042

L1020

L1035

L1036

L1042

(Conshohocken, PA) 1970-71; and Skyway Products, Inc. (Brooklyn, NY) 1972-73.

K5000 KNIVES, POCKET

Imperial Knife made Mickey Mouse knives in the 30's and Davy Crockett styles in the 50's. An early enameled pen knife looks to have been made by Cohn & Rosenberger.

K5010	Knife, enameled	20 - 200
K5020	Mickey pen knife, 2 styles, Imperial	5 - 70
K5022	Mickey 2 blade knife, Imperial	10 - 85
K5023	Mickey 4 blade knife, Imperial	15 - 125
K5040	Davy Crockett Frontier knife	5 - 25
K5041	Davy Tomahawk knife with caplifter	6 - 30
K5042	Davy 3 blade Frontier Knife	5 - 28

Licensed manufacturer — The Imperial Knife Co. (Providence, RI) 1936-38, 55-59.

Also see SILVERWARE and FLATWEAR.

L1000 LAMPS, LAMPSHADES AND NIGHTLIGHTS

There are many classic Disney lamps. Finding one with its original shade is rare. The extra wide price spreads in this section take this factor into consideration. The top price is for a mint lamp with a fine to mint grade original shade, except for night lights that had no shade.

L1010	Krueger musical 3 Pigs lamp (1933)	25 - 250
Soreng-Manegold Company (L1020-L1028)		
L1020	Mickey lamps, green or tan, 3 shade styles, each	7 - 70
L1023	Same as L1020 (1935), but new shade (1936)	7 - 70
L1025	Mickey or Donald wall lamp, each	8 - 85
L1027	Mickey in chair	30 - 350
L1028	Donald standing at post	35 - 400
L1030	Mickey, Donald or Dopey battery operated "Kiddy-Lites" (Micro-Lite) each	8 - 65
L1034	Dopey at kettle (LaMode)	25 - 145
L1035	Snow White at wishing well (LaMode)	25 - 145
L1036	Snow White, Dopey, Grumpy, Doc, Mickey or Donald plaster lamp and shade (LaMode), each	12 - 95
L1042	Bookend lamps or night-lites (LaMode), same characters as L1036, each	15 - 110
L1048	Same characters as bookends only, each set of 2	15 - 60
L1050	Multi-Products Pinocchio, Jiminy Crickett, Geppetto, Lampwick figures, Flexo table lamp, each	10 - 100
L1054	Multi-Products wall plaques (3) Flexo wall lamps, each	10 - 100
L1063	Mickey, Minnie, Donald, Joe Carioca, Panchito (Evan K. Shaw design) or Dopey table lamps, each	15 - 150

L1050   L1054

L1027   L1028

L1034

L1048   L1074   L1074

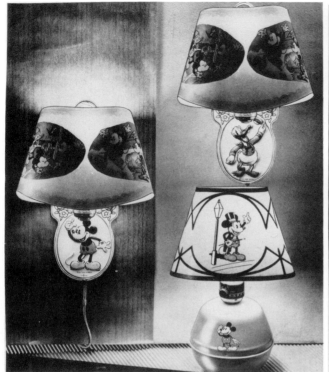

L1025   L1023

L1030

L1200

L1063

L2501

L2670

L1069

L2600

L1069	Snow White's Bluebirds, Donald or Pluto wall lamps (Railley), each	12 - 120
L1074	Donald, Dopey and others Leeds China designs, each	10 - 70
L1200	Snow White nite-lite (Hankscraft)	10 - 55

Licensed manufacturers- Clevelite Products Inc. (Cleveland, OH) 1946-48; Doris Lamp Shades, Inc. (NYC) 1938-39, shades only; Econolite Corp. (LA) 1955-57; Flexo Products (Chicago) 1940-41; General Electric Co. Wiring Device Dept. (Warwick, RI) 1968-84, wall socket nite-lites; Globe Lighting Products, Inc. (Brooklyn, NY) 1947-49; Hankscraft Co. (Reedsburg, WI) 1959; La Mode Studios, Inc. (NYC) 1938-39; Micro-Lite Co., Inc. (NYC) 1938-40; Nathan Lagin Co. (NYC) 1940-41; Norman Industries, Inc. (LA) 1970-74; Plastimatic, Inc. (Norwood, NJ) 1982-84; Railley Corp. (Cleveland, OH) 1947-48; Royalty Designs, Inc. (Miami, FL) 1954-56, Lady and the Tramp and Davy Crockett lamps; Solar Electric Corp. (Warren, PA) 1956-57, bulbs and lamp bases; Soreng-Manegold Co. (Chicago) 1934-38; The Straits Corp. (Detroit) 1934-35, shades only; Studio Design, Inc. (Rainbow Art Glass) (Neptune, NJ) 1979-83 Tiffany style lamp, wall light and shade kits; and Universal Lamp Co., Inc. (Chicago) 1970-71, blow molded lamps.

L2000 LANTERNS, MAGIC AND SLIDES

There was a Mickey Mouse Toy Lantern Outfit made by Ensign, Ltd. under an English license. The boxed sets show up at major toy shows for 150 - 250 in complete fine to mint condition. The small boxes of glass "full color" slides (extra "shows" sold separately) go for 10 - 40 each.

L2500 LEEDS CHINA COMPANY

Leeds China Company (Chicago) was a licensee from 1944-1954. Flower shops were major customers. Planters and pitchers with flower arrangements were basic products. The product line was diverse. (see BANKS, COOKIE JARS, PITCHERS and SALT AND PEPPER SHAKERS) Earlier pieces were painted overglaze and the paint flaked off. Later pieces were airbrushed with lighter pastel colors under glaze. These remain in excellent condition, but are seen less often. Lamp bases were perhaps made for a different manufacturer. The designs seem endless. Paint variations add to the variety. Some are even edged in gold. Assortments for 1947 and 1949 are pictured along with some individual pieces. Prices are listed by category.

L2501	Figurines, overglaze, each	4 - 25
L2530	Figurines, underglaze, each	5 - 30
L2560	Planters, overglaze, each	3 - 18
L2600	Planters, underglaze, each	3 - 25
L2670	Childs feeding dishes	8 - 40

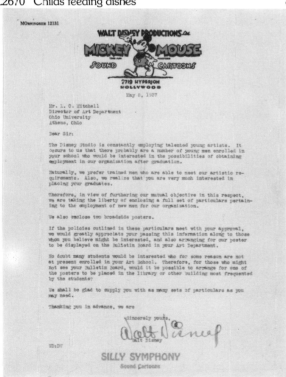

L4000

L2530   L2600   L2560

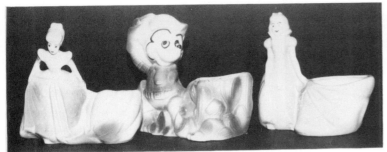

L2600

L4600

L4600

L8500

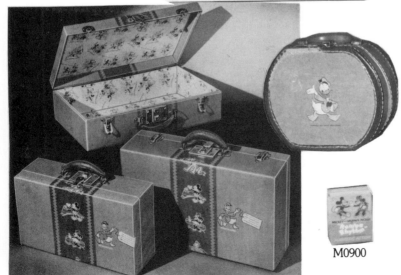

L8500

M0900

L5000

L4000 LETTERHEADS

Company letterhead stationery comes in two main forms. Those 1) used to conduct business by Studio, theme park, or other operation or 2) used to promote a film. The latter are more colorful and plentiful. Letters signed by Disney employees were often kept and turn up regularly to provide a history of corporate letterhead. Most fall into the 1 - 10 range. Older Studio stationery brings 5 - 15. A letter authentically signed by Walt brings 150 and up depending on the nature of the letter.

L4600 LICENSE PLATES

There have been two types of theme park souvenir license plates. Disneyland U. S. A. had a series of 6 bicycle type in the 60's. Value 1 - 8 each. Regular size plates have been issued since around 1978 for each theme park and some special events. Value 1 - 10 each.

L5000 LOBBY CARDS

A set of lobby cards, usually 8, is issued with each release of a Disney film. The design of the title card in each set changes with each re-release. Other cards may change or ones from a previous release re-used. They are printed and in color vs. still photos that are usually black and white. The standard size is 11″ x 14″. Older animation sets sell well at film collector conventions. Sets from animation films since *Lady and the Tramp* go for 10 - 40 in their illustrated envelopes. Individual animated feature lobby cards can be found for .50 - 4 each.

L8500 LUGGAGE, BRIEFCASES, TOTE BAGS, ETC.

Children's character luggage in one form or another has been made since 1934. It's not exciting or very collectible, but older pieces can bring up to 35 - 40. Pieces from the 40's to present command 1 - 15.

Licensed manufacturers — AMSCO Industries, Inc. division of Milton Bradley (Warminster, PA) 1972+; Burlington Luggage Co., Inc. (Seattle, WA) 1945-48; Butterfly Originals (Cherry Hill, NJ) 1976-77; Evans-Aristocrat Industries, Inc. (NYC) 1972; Hollywood Luggage Co. (LA) 1947-48; Ideal Toy Company (Hollis, NY) 1968; Monroe Luggage Co., Inc. (NYC) 1938-39; Neevel Mfg. Co. (Kansas City, MO) 1949-56; Prepac, Inc. (Bronx, NY) 1975-80; Seattle Luggage Corp. (Seattle, WA) 1947-48, same products as Hollywood Luggage Co.; Seward Luggage Co. (Dayton, OH) 1975; Standard Briefcase Co., Inc. (NYC) 1934-35 and A D Sutton & Sons (NYC) 1970-72.

L9000 LUNCH BOXES AND KITS

Four licensees have provided an almost continuous supply of lunch boxes in non-war years. Each one since the 50's came with a thermos bottle. Prices are for complete units. Scratches and rust rapidly deplete value.

L9005	Mickey Mouse Lunch Kit (1935-37)	15 - 175
L9008	Snow White lunch box (Libbey)	5 - 40
L9010	Pinocchio lunch box (Libbey)	4 - 35
L9011	Pinocchio lunch pail (Libbey)	5 - 40
L9025	Mickey/Donald (Liberty)	4 - 25
L9026	Davy Crockett (Liberty)	4 - 25
L9030	Disney School Bus	3 - 15
L9031	Disney Fire Engine	3 - 20

Aladdin Industries has participated in virtually every major Disney promotional event since 1956 with a metal or plastic lunch kit.

L4000

L9010

L9025

L9005

L9100

L9035

L9150

M1000

M1000

L9035 Aladdin lunch kits, 50's	3 - 20
L9100 Aladdin lunch kits, 60's	3 - 15
L9150 Aladdin lunch kits, 70's	2 - 8
L9200 Aladdin lunch kits, 80's	1 - 4

Licensed manufacturers — Aladdin Industries, Inc. (Nashville, TN) 1956-85; Geuder, Paeschke & Frey Co. (Milwaukee, WI) 1935-37; Libbey Glass Company division of Owens-Illinois (Toledo, OH) 1938-41; and Liberty National Corp. (NYC) 1954-56.

M0900 MAGNETS AND MAGNETIC NOVELTIES

The Rhumba Rhythm of Mickey and Minnie Mouse is the only vintage piece in this class, and is worth 2 - 10. The others are refrigerator magnets sold as theme park souvenirs or by plastic novelty companies. Value .10 - .50 each.

Licensed manufacturer — Masco Corp. (Chicago) 1946-48.

M1000 MAGAZINE ARTICLES

The Disney Studio honeymoon with magazine publishers lasted Walt Disney's lifetime. Articles were different, colorful, and of public interest. The history they provide is vast. Movie magazines of the 30's did regular features on Mickey Mouse and other shorts, plus the features beginning with *Snow White*. During the 40's it was "Walt Disney Goes to War" and colorful story boards of animated films. *The Saturday Evening Post* did two series on Walt Disney in the 50's — "The Amazing Story of Walt Disney" and the serialization of his daughter Diane Disney Miller's book, entitled "My Dad, Walt Disney." *Life* magazine did an article on collecting Disneyana in the 60's. There were hundreds if not thousands of articles in various publications. A few collectors specialize in collecting this inexpensive material. The earliest articles run only 10 - 20 and a black and white copy of most of these would do. Color became a factor around Snow White, but so much of this material was saved. Most 40's articles can be purchased for 2 - 10 with whole magazines from the 50's and 60's selling for 1 - 5.

Also see GOOD HOUSEKEEPING CHILDREN'S PAGES

M2000 MAGAZINES WITH DISNEY COVERS

So strong was the appeal of a Disney article, many were cover stories. *Colliers* and *Liberty* magazines often used Disney characters on the cover when no major article appeared. In this case, usually the whole issue is collected. Framing a nice selection is also attractive. The March 14, 1942 issue of *Liberty* depicts one of the few publicity uses of Mickey with dimensional ears. Expect to pay 3 - 25 for a magazine with a good Disney cover.

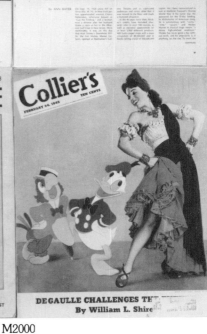

M2000

111

M2000

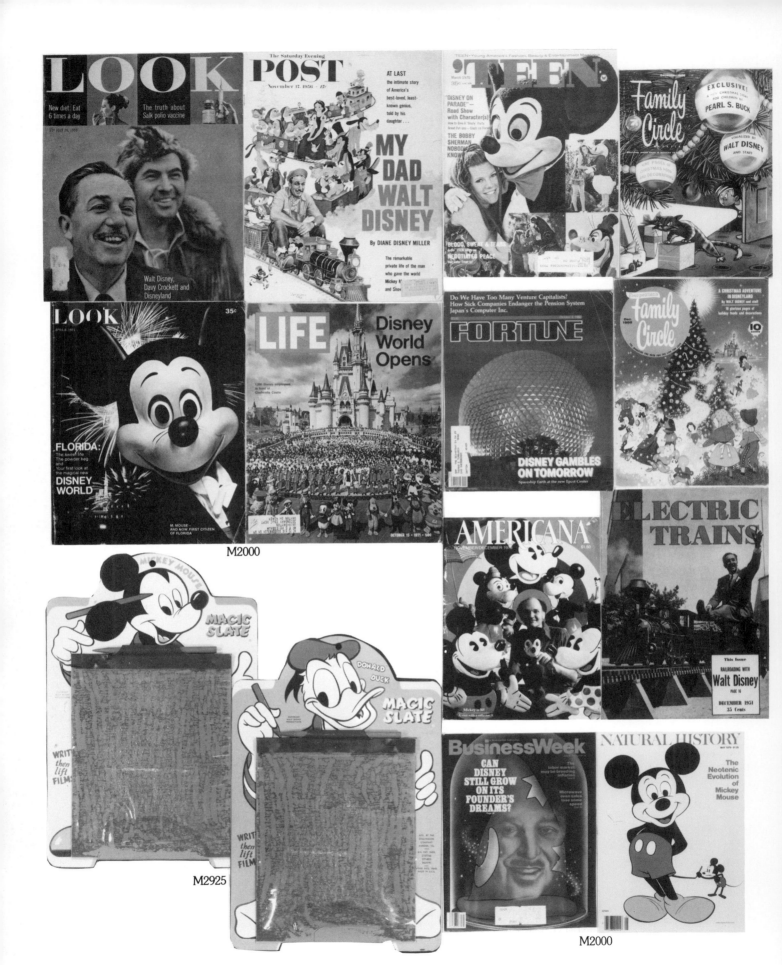

M2000

M2925

M2000

M2900 MAGIC SLATES

There was a "white slate" forerunner (1936) to the Strathmore Company's "magic slates" that proved popular in the 40's and 50's. Whitman took over the production of magic slates in 1970.

M2910	Mickey Mouse White Slate (Platt & Munk)	10 - 45
M2920	Magic slate Blackboard (Strathmore)	8 - 38
M2925	Mickey or Donald Magic Slate (Strathmore)	4 - 15
M2935	Mickey Mouse Club Magic Slate TV Activity Book series — Jiminy Cricket Magic Slate, Mickey Mouse Club Drawing Fun, Jimmie Dodd Magic Slate, and Spin and Marty Triple "R" Magic Slate (Strathmore), each	3 - 12
M2940	Davy Crockett Magic Slate	4 - 15
M2942	Zorro TV Action Magic Slate game	5 - 20
M2945	The Sword in the Stone (Watkins-Strathmore)	3 - 12
M2960	Whitman Magic Slates	1 - 5

Licensed manufacturers — The Platt & Munk Co., Inc. (NYC) 1936-37; Strathmore Company (Aurora, IL) 1943-46, 55-58; Watkins-Strathmore (Racine, WI) 1963, 68; and Whitman Publishing Company (Racine, WI) 1970-85.

M2940

M2945

M2910

To retail at $1.00

M3000 MAPS

The Globe Trotter map (See BREAD CARDS AND PREMIUMS) was the first good Disney map. Dixon pencil boxes enclosed a character map of the U. S. in larger pencil boxes. Standard Oil Company of California came out with Mickey & Donald's Race to Treasure Island — a tie-in promotion with the Golden Gate International Exposition on San Francisco Bay (Travel-Tykes Weekly contained stamps for this map). There was Peter Pan's map of Neverland in 1952 and the first map of Disneyland in 1958 (See DISNEYLAND). Other theme park maps followed.

M3008	Dixon pencil box maps	10 - 60
M3020	Race to Treasure Island (Standard) with stamps	15 - 150
M3021	Race to Treasure Island (Calso) with stamps	20 - 200

M3008

M2920

M2935

M3028

LOOK FOR ALL THE WALT DISNEY FUN MASKS

DONALD DUCK   CINDERELLA   LUCIFER

BRER RABBIT   MICKEY MOUSE

PINOCCHIO   BAMBI

COMPLETE SET—8 IN ALL!

M3131

M3131

M3131

M3131

M3021

M3120

114

M3028 Peter Pan's map of Neverland (Colgate Peter
    Pan Beauty Bar)   15 - 150
Licensed manufacturers — Jos. Dixon Crucible Co. (Jersey City, NJ)
1931-42; Peter Pan Beauty Bar (Colgate-Jersey City, NJ) 1952; Standard
Oil Company of California, 1939-49; and Vicks Chemical Co. (NYC)
1956, Official Mickey Mouse World Reporter press card, badge, and
map (supplied by Rand McNally).

M3100 MASKS

Einson-Freeman made paper masks since 1933. Masquerade
costume makers supplied masks with each costume (See COS-
TUMES AND PLAY OUTFITS). Procter and Gamble offered
Snow White and the 7 Dwarfs premium masks in 1938. Gillette
did likewise with Pinocchio. Wheaties offered 8 Disney masks
on package backs in 1950 and others.

M3104 Mickey or Minnie (Einson-Freeman), each   10 - 40
M3108 Snow White set (Procter & Gamble), each   5 - 15
    Whitman Snow White mask book (see B3107)
M3120 Pinocchio set (Gillette), each   2 - 8
M3130 Donald (Donald Duck Bread) 1949   2 - 8
M3131 Wheaties — Mickey, Donald, Dumbo, Cinderella,
    Lucifer, Br'er Rabbit, Pinocchio or Bambi, each   2 - 10
Licensed manufacturers — Einson-Freeman Company (Long Island
City, NY) 1933-34, 39; General Mills (Minneapolis, MN) 1950; Gillette
Safety Razor Company (Pinocchio/Blue Blades promotion) 1940-41;
Rubber for Molds, Inc. (Chicago) 1948-49; and Space Face (Laguna
Hills, CA) 1983.

M3900 MERCHANDISE CATALOGS

Kay Kamen initially went to work as Roy and Walt Disney's
special representative for character merchandising. United Artists issued an exhibitors campaign book in 1932 and a series of
special Christmas promotion books were published. When sub-
licensing contracts with Borgfeldt and Levy ran out (See The
Disney Time Line — Vol. 1) Kamen became sole character
licensing agent and issued the first real merchandise catalog in
1934. The other issues were 1935, 1936-37, 1938-39. 1940-41,
1947-48 and 1949-50. Following Kamen's death, the company
reclaimed all merchandising rights and issued catalogs on a film-
by-film basis. Walt Disney Distributing Co. was formed in 1971
and operated until 1977. They issued one catalog, portfolios of
catalog pages, and then looseleaf catalogs. Magic Kingdom Club
and theme park mail order catalogs are condensed, but provide
some reference.

M3901 United Artists campaign book   150 - 500
M3902 Christmas Promotion Books   30 - 300
M3910 Merchandise Catalogs (Kamen)   150 - 500
M3920 Merchandise division catalogs   5 - 20
M3970 Walt Disney Distributing Co. catalogs   10 - 25

M3104

M3108

M3130

M3910

CHRISTMAS PROMOTION 1934

CHRISTMAS PROMOTION 1935

CHRISTMAS PROMOTION 1936

M3902

CHRISTMAS PROMOTION

AFTER SNOW WHITE ...WHAT?

M3910

M3910

M3910

M3920

M3970

M3970

M4502

M4504

M4601

M4505

116

M4500 MICKEY MOUSE CLUBS

The first Mickey Mouse Club was created in Sept. 1929 by Harry W. Woodin, manager of the Fox Dome Theater in Ocean Park, CA. He later joined the Disney organization to create clubs in theaters across the nation. A typical club meeting was held at noon on Saturday before the matinee. There was a club meeting with merchant tie-ins, contests, prizes, and giveaways. Officers received special badges and conducted meetings. They changed every 8 weeks. Theaters paid only $25 plus supplies. They received a General Campaign book, Club song sheets, officer badges, etc. The club drummed home good behavior, got kids involved with theaters and merchants, didn't cost much and was a huge success. At its peak in 1932 the national Mickey Mouse club had over a million members from over 800 theaters each with memberships in the 1,000 to 5,000 range. In fact, it was becoming too difficult to handle and it was decided to let the clubs die a natural death. That took till the 1950's in one Florida theater. The second Mickey Mouse Club was the ABC television version. It first aired Oct 3, 1955 and became a national phenomenon. SFM Entertainment acquired the rights to syndicate the black and white TV episodes in the mid-70's. The success they enjoyed led to the creation of the New Mickey Mouse Club in Jan 1977 after a "nationwide" talent search. It didn't click and was cancelled in its second season. The logos of the second and third clubs are similar. In some cases the 50's logo was used on 70's merchandise. The earliest design has a large "M" around Mickey's head and the word Mouseketeers. The 3rd club had open face, bold letters spelling out the words Mickey Mouse Club. Listed at this classification are Club promotion items, membership cards and a few items that fit in. Toys, magazines, pinback buttons, etc. are found at other classifications.

First Mickey Mouse Club — Movie Theaters 1929-35

M4501 General Campaign manual	50 - 250
M4502 Membership application	2 - 8
M4503 Membership card	3 - 20
M4504 Birthday card	3 - 25
M4505 Promotional banners or supplies	5 - 500
M4506 Reproductions of M4505 signs	2 - 10
M4515 Newsletters	10 - 80

ABC Television Mickey Mouse Club 1955-59 and reruns

M4600 Membership application or card	1 - 10
M4601 Membership card/certificate mailer	2 - 15
M4625 Mouseketeer Cast Photo Album	3 - 18

Regular licensees such as Whitman, Aladdin (lunch boxes) and a few others supported the 3rd Club, but there was no real organization as there had been in the two previous ventures. Items produced aren't very collectible as they were cheaply made and sold by the pound at deep discount prices when the show was cancelled.

Licensed manufacturers — Savoy-Reeland Printing Co. (NYC) 1931, printers of Mickey Mouse Club materials and Fisch & Co., Inc. (LA) 1931-33, makers of pants, caps, banners, and felt pennants.

M4900 MICKEY MOUSE CLUB MAGAZINES AND ANNUALS

Volume one of the official Club magazine was issued quarterly before it became a bi-monthly publication in Dec 1956.

M4501

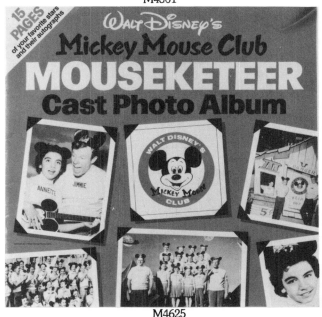

M4625

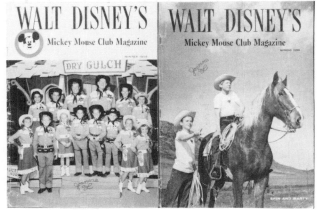

M4901   M4902

M4903   M4904

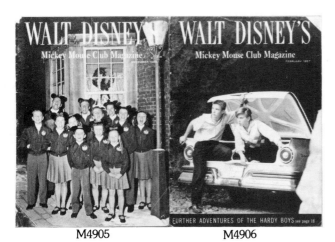

M4905   M4906

M4907   M4908

M4909   M4910

M4913   M4914

M4915   M4916

M4917   M4918

M4919   M4920

M4921   M4922

Seven issues were titled Walt Disney's Mickey Mouse Club Magazine before the name was shortened to Walt Disney's Magazine. The last six issues were smaller. Ads show many Mickey Mouse Club toys and premiums. Annuals reprint earlier magazines.

M4901	Volume 1 — Number 1 (Winter 1956)	5 - 50
M4902	Volume 1 — Number 2 (Spring 1956)	5 - 45
M4903	Volume 1 — Number 3 (Summer 1956)	4 - 40
M4904	Volume 1 — Number 4 (Fall 1956)	4 - 40
M4905	Volume 2 — Number 1 (December 1956)	3 - 30
M4906	Volume 2 — Number 2 through Volume 2 — Number 6, each	2 - 20
M4913	Volume 3 — Number 1 through Volume 3 — Number 6, each	2 - 10
M4919	Volume 4 — Number 1 through Volume 4 — Number 6 (Oct 59), each	1 - 8
M4926	Annual #1	2 - 20
M4927	Annual #2	1 - 15

Licensed manufacturer — Western Printing and Lithographing Co. (Poughkeepsie, NY) 1956-59, Annuals Whitman division.

M5000 MICKEY MOUSE EARS

Mouseketeer Ears originated with the 1955 TV show, but have been sold at Disneyland and throughout the world ever since in endless varieties. Originals have felt ears; later models, thin plastic ears. Some were "ear" headbands, others had moveable ears. Ears can be found with theme park, Mouse Factory, Disney on Parade, Disney ice shows, the Disney Channel, and other logos. One could specialize in collecting Mouse Ears. They are reasonably priced at about 5 - 15 for older unique 50's models. Special logo ears go for 3 - 10. Others for 1 - 5.

Licensed manufacturers — Benay-Albee Novelty Co., Inc. (Maspeth, NY) 1956-59, felt hat ears with big M logo; Empire Plastics Corp. (Tarboro, NC) 1956, same plastic ear headband as produced by Kohner Brothers (NYC) 1956; Welded Plastics Corp. (NYC) 1955-56, Plastic mousecaps with moveable ears.

M4923   M4924

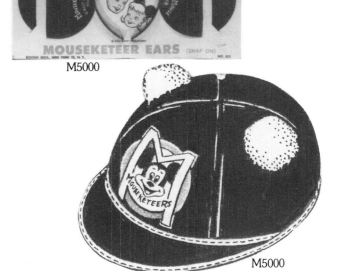

M4926   M4927

Hi MOUSEKETEER!

M4600

M5000

MOUSEKETEER EARS (SNAP ON)

M5000

M5000

M5000

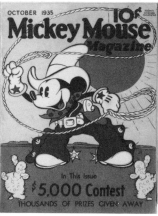

M5436

M5435

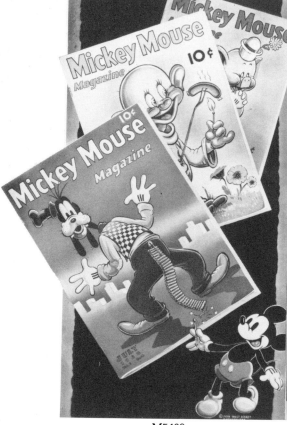

M5444

M5400

M5437

M5400 MICKEY MOUSE MAGAZINES

The first series of Mickey Mouse Magazines (9) — Vol. 1, No. 1 (Jan 33) thru Vol 1, No. 9 (Sept 33) — was distributed through theaters and department stores. A new series beginning Nov 33 was part of Kay Kamen's dairy campaign. There were 24 giveaway issues — two volumes of 12 each — ending with the Oct 35 publication. The second series was published by Hal Horne, Inc. (NYC) The third series was sold on newsstands for 10¢ each (except #1 and Dec 36 Christmas issues — sold for 25¢ each). The initial Summer issue (released May 1935) and the eight following were produced by Hal Horne (Monthly except Jan 36 — no issue). Kay Kamen took over after the June 36 number and managed the magazine through its conversion to Walt Disney's Comics and Stories in Oct 1940. The magazine changed sizes three times — after the 1st, 2nd and Aug 1939 issue. The newsstand version had great art and many ads for early Disneyana.

M5411

M5410   M5412

M5422

M5401	First series Jan-Sept 1933, each	15 - 100
M5410	Dairy series # 1, Nov 1933	10 - 90
M5411	Dairy # 2, Dec 1933	8 - 75
M5412	Dairy #s 3 - 12, Jan 34 - Oct 34, each	7 - 50
M5422	Dairy #s 13 - 24, Nov 34 - Oct 35, each	6 - 35
M5435	Newsstand #1, Summer (May) 1935	30 - 300
M5436	Newsstand #2, Oct 1935	25 - 250
M5437	Newsstand #3, Nov 35 - #9, June 36, each	15 - 150
M5444	Newsstand #10, July 36 - #61, Sept 40, each	10 - 90

M5500 MICKEY MOUSE WEEKLY

Mickey Mouse Weekly was published in England. The first issue (11" x 15") appeared Feb 8, 1936 and continued to 1959. Thousands of these issues have found their way to the U. S. They sell in the 10 - 20 range, except for the very early numbers.

M6200 MILK BOTTLES AND COLLARS

Owens-Illinois Pacific Coast Co. (San Francisco) was licensed to produce "glass containers" for 1936-37. The Owens-Illinois Can Company (Toledo, OH) took over for the years 1938-41. Pint, half-pint, and quart bottles were produced featuring the main cartoon characters and those from Snow White, Ferdinand the Bull, and Pinocchio. Nearly 40 different straight and creamer designs are known. Images on the bottles aren't paint or ink — rather molten color glass. Valued at 75 - 125 each. The Wolf Envelope Co. (Cleveland, OH), a major producer of paper advertising collars that slipped over the neck of the bottle before capping, was licensed to use Disney characters from 1939-41. The author is not aware of the existence or value of these collars.

M6300 MIRRORS

Theodore Diamond introduced a classic series of Mickey Mouse mirrors in 1936. Galax Minor Company was licensed for 1938-39 and there have been many producers of theme park merchandise.

M6310	Theodore Diamond, 3 designs, each	20 - 80
M6315	Galax mirrors, each	15 - 70
M6335	Mirrors, 50's and later, each	5 - 35

Licensed manufacturers — Barnett Mirror Corp. (Bronx, NY) 1957-58; mirrors, mirror toys and mirror furniture; Bassett Mirror Co. (Basset, VA) 1968, 1977-79; Russ Berrie & Co. (Oakland, NJ) 1975-76; novelty wall mirrors; Theodore Diamond, Inc. (NYC) 1936-37; Galax Mirror Co. (Galax, VA) 1938-39; Mechanical Mirror Works, Inc. (NYC) 1977-81; shadow boxes, glass greeting cards, and framed glass wall decorations; Sculptors Guild Ltd. (St. Louis, MO) 1981-83, sculptured mirrors with and without stained glass; and Sentinel Plastics division of Gulf & Western Corp. (Bronx, NY) 1972-74.

Also see — HAIR BRUSHES, COMBS AND ACCESSORIES

M6400 MOBILES

There have been numerous consumer products mobiles designed for the baby's crib and as party decorations. A large number have also been produced for film promotion. Value 5 - 25 each.

Licensed manufacturers — Kinner Products Co. (Cincinnati, OH) 1959; Sears, Roebuck & Co. (Chicago) 1964; Simon & Schuster (NYC) 1955; and U. S. Plastics Company (Pasadena, CA) 1954-55.

M6500 MODEL KITS

Revell, a leading name in model airplane and car kits, and other

M5400

M5500

M6200

0553-9190
Mickey Mouse Mirror
12¼" x 18¼"

0553-9193
Wayward Canary Mirror
12¼" x 18¼"

0553-9191
Spirit of 76 Mirror
12¼" x 18¼"

0553-9189
Mickey's Pal Mirra-mat
8" x 10" Picture Frame

0553-9195
Mickey's Pal Pluto
(not shown) 12¼" x 18¼"

0553-9194
The Whoopee Party Mirror
12¼" x 18¼"

0553-9192
Mickey's Nightmare Mirror
12¼" x 18¼"

WALT DISNEY DISTRIBUTING CO.
General Office: P.O. Box 40, Lake Buena Vista, Florida 32830
(305/828-2411)

PRINTED IN U.S.A.   ©1976 WALT DISNEY PRODUCTIONS

M6335

M6310

M6400

M6335

manufacturers have produced some unusual Disney model kits over the years. These are all figural when constructed, but specialized collectors search for unassembled kits in the original boxes.

M6525	Perri the Squirrel	5 - 50
M6527	Tomorrowland Rocket	6 - 60
M6528	Peter Pan's Pirate Ship (from Disneyland)	8 - 75
M6530	Sleeping Beauty, the Prince and Sampson	5 - 50
M6550	The Robin Hood Characters (5)	3 - 15
M6551	The Royal Coach, Elephant and Prince John	3 - 15

Pirates of the Caribbean "Zap-action" models (MPC)

M6555	Ghosts of the Treasure Guard	2 - 10
M6556	Dead Men Tell No Tales	2 - 10
M6557	Dead Man's Raft	3 - 12
M6558	Hoist High the Jolly Roger	2 - 10
M6559	Condemned to Chains Forever	3 - 12
M6560	Fate of the Mutineers	2 - 10
M6561	Freed in the Nick of Time	3 - 12

Licensed manufacturers — Milton Bradley Co. (Springfield, MA) 1977-79, building blocks models; Model Products Co. (Mt. Clemens, MI) 1972-79; Revell, Inc. (Venice, CA) 1957-59, 70-74; Strombeck-Becker Mfg. Co. (Moline, IL) 1955-59, Mickey Mouse and Davy Crockett stagecoach model kit; and Testor Corp. (LA) 1981-82.

H1765

M6400

M6525

M6557

M6561

M6528

M6558

M6550

M6559

M6551

MPC plastic models from The Black Hole. *Value 2-10 each.*

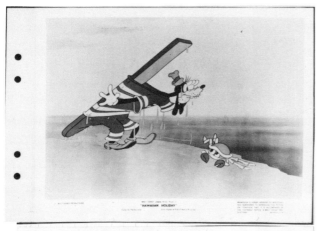

M7000

M7000

M7000 MOVIE STILLS

Movie stills are created for publicity purposes, but are displayed in theaters as well. The size is normally 8″ x 10″. Older stills that came from studio still books had cloth backs and a binding tab. Stills are abundant for features and newer shorts. Most are black and white, but there were some early tinted stills and colored ones are routine for post-50's films. Value .50 - 2, each. Older cartoon stills are rarer, but are easily reproduced. This has tended to keep values down. The value of tinted and rarer cartoon stills must be judged on an individual basis.

Also see — LOBBY CARDS.

M8500 MUGS

Mugs or coffee cups are often included in chinaware or dinner sets. The ones at this class are more along the line of individual milk or coffee mugs. There have been hundreds. Those listed are a mere representation. The majority are theme park vintage.

M8510	30's earthenware beer mugs, each	8 - 60
M8520	40's glass or ceramic mugs, each	4 - 25
M8530	50's glass, ceramic, or plastic, each	2 - 15
M8540	60's glass, ceramic, or plastic, each	2 - 10
M8550	70's glass, ceramic, or plastic, each	1 - 8
M8560	80's glass, ceramic, or plastic, each	1 - 4

Licensed manufacturers — Admiral Plastics Corp. (Brooklyn, NY) 1968-80; Dan Brechner & Co., Inc. (NYC) 1961-63; California Originals (Torrance, CA) 1979; Enesco Imports, Inc. (Chicago) 1968-71; Haroco (Skokie, IL) 1980; Hazel-Atlas Glass Co. (Wheeling, WV) 1955, mugs, cereal dishes and saucers for Ogilvie Flour Mills Co., Ltd. of Canada; U. S. American (LA) 1983-84; among others.

Also see — CHINAWARE, DINNERWARE and SILVER-WARE.

M8510

M7000

Salem China mugs — see CHINAWARE

M8530   M8540

M8550

M8550

125

Decorative Gifts

Mickey Mouse Club   0553-0356

0553-0338   Mickey Pedestal Mug

0553-0326   Mickey Milk Mug

0553-0339   Snow White

0553-0324   Alice In Wonderland

0553-0336   Lady & Tramp

Porcelain Mugs

0553-0323   Aristocats

0553-0335   Character Parade

0553-0322   Jungle Book

0553-9077   Milk Mug Set, 5 Piece

0553-9075   Cake Set, 4 Piece

0553-9076   Pedestal Mug Set, 5 Piece

Packaged Porcelain Mug and Cake Sets   Each Set Assorted Characters Mickey, Donald, Pluto, Dopey

WALT DISNEY DISTRIBUTING CO.
General Office: P.O. Box 40, Lake Buena Vista, Florida 32830
(305/828-2411)

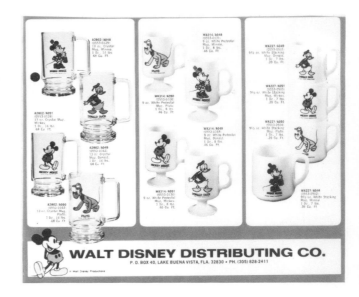

WALT DISNEY DISTRIBUTING CO.
P.O. BOX 40, LAKE BUENA VISTA, FLA. 32830 • PH. (305) 828-2411

Decorative Gifts

3 Little Pig Musicals play "Who's Afraid of the Big Bad Wolf".

Snow White Musical plays "Someday My Prince Will Come"

0553-9504   Big Bad Wolf Figurine, Bisque 6"

0553-9503   Snow White Musical, Bisque 7½"

0553-9501   Fiddler Pig Musical, Bisque 6"

0553-9502   Practical Pig Musical, Bisque 6"

0553-9500   Fifer Pig Musical, Bisque 6"

M9195

M9100

M9025

M9050

M9000 MUSIC BOXES

It seems there should be many old music boxes from the 30's and 40's, but there don't appear to have been any music "boxes" marketed in the U. S. until the Chein Disneyland "Melody Player" in 1955. Jaymar did a rather tacky musical jewelry box in 1970 — also the year Schmid Brothers, Inc., the largest manufacturer of Disney music boxes, became a licensee. There have been several porcelain bisque music boxes sold at theme parks. Grolier Enterprises has a Musical Memory bisque music box series of the major Disney animated features.

M9025 Disneyland "Melody Player"	15 - 75
M9026 Extra rolls for M9025 each	2 - 8
M9031 Small World doll mount (1963-64)	5 - 20
M9035 Jewelry box with pop-up Mickey (Jaymar) 1970	1 - 8
M9040 Small World, plastic suitcase	2 - 10

The first Schmid music boxes were wooden character scenes. By 1973, the line included musical key rings, blocks, mugs, plus Christmas collectors' plates. All music boxes were then ceramic, including Mickey and Pinocchio wall hanging units. The Schmid line continued to broaden over the next several years to include thimbles, figurines, bells, collectors' plates for other occasions, plus animated and figural music boxes and musical picture frames. Character, tune and design variations are extensive while values remain largely in the same ranges.

M9050 Wooden music boxes, each (1970-71)	15 - 65
M9060 Musical key chains, each	6 - 25
M9070 Musical blocks, each	10 - 40
M9080 Musical mugs, each	7 - 30
M9100 Ceramic revolving, Mickey (3 versions), Minnie, Donald (3 versions), Bambi, Winnie the Pooh, Cinderella, Pinocchio, and Pluto, each	10 - 35
M9115 Mickey or Pinocchio, wall hanging	15 - 50

Major additions were made to the Schmid music box line in 1976. In addition to two Bicentennial designs (See AMERICA ON PARADE), Mickey's birthday cake, Snow White, each of the Seven Dwarfs, and Goofy were added.

M9122 Snow White or Seven Dwarfs, each	10 - 35
M9130 Goofy	10 - 35
M9135 Aristocat characters — Scat Cat, Italian Cat, Duchess, O'Malley, and 1 other, each (1980)	12 - 38

Six different Winnie the Pooh character activity music boxes were introduced in 1981.

M9140 Winnie the Pooh characters — Christopher Robin/ Pooh, Tigger/Pooh, Pooh/Piglet, Pooh/Eeyore, Pooh/Rabbit or Kanga/Roo, each	12 - 38
M9146 3 Pigs	10 - 35
M9147 Mickey on Ice, Mickey Soccer, Mickey Tennis, Mickey Baseball, Mickey on Skis, Donald Golf, Mickey Dancing, Mickey Golf, or Mickey Surf, each	10 - 35
M9160 Mickey or Minnie musical photo frames, each	5 - 18
M9165 Mickey, Minnie or Pinocchio figural, large, each	25 - 75
M9168 Articulated figural, Mickey, Minnie, Pinocchio, Donald, Jiminy Cricket or Pig, each	15 - 40
M9175 Snow White or Cinderella figural, each	12 - 38
M9177 Snow White or Cinderella, revolving, each	10 - 30
M9179 Seven Dwarfs, new design, each	10 - 30
M9190 Mickey/train, Minnie/doll, Donald or Pinocchio/ hobby horses, Dumbo, Bambi, Thumper, or Jiminy Cricket, each (1984)	10 - 25
M9195 Snow White, Practical Pig, Fifer Pig or Fiddler Pig theme park bisque music boxes, each	10 - 30

Licensed manufacturers — J. Chein & Co., Inc. (Newark, NJ) 1953-55; Diablo Products Corp. (Concord, CA) 1982-84, Musical light switch; Jaymar Specialty Co. (Brooklyn, NY) 1970-?; and Schmid Brothers, Inc. (Boston, MA) 1970-85.

M9500 MUSICAL INSTRUMENTS

Borgfeldt started a line of wind instruments in 1935. Noble & Cooley provided drums, banjos and tambourines. Davy Crockett had a guitar and there was a flood of Mousegetars in conjunction with the TV Mickey Mouse Club.

M9505 Trumpet, trombone, clarinet or saxophone

M9177

M9175   M9179

M9190

M9168

M9540

M9616

M9562

M9535

M9552

M9546

M9558

N1520

M9545

N2500

(Borgfeldt), each	6 - 60
M9509 Harmonica (Borgfeldt)	5 - 35
M9520 Drums, trap set (N & C)	25 - 125
M9521 Illustrated 14" drum (N & C)	8 - 80
M9522 Illustrated 7" drum (N & C)	5 - 50
M9523 Banjo, illustrated (N & C)	5 - 50
M9524 Tamborine, illustrated (N & C)	4 - 30
M9532 Metal drums, various sizes (Ohio Art)	6 - 60
M9535 Lido plastic slide whistles, each	2 - 8
M9540 Mickey Mouse Rhythm Band (Emenee)	5 - 50
M9542 Davy Crockett guitar, in case (PPP)	5 - 50
M9545 Mousegetar, 23" (Mattel)	3 - 30
M9546 Mousegetar, Jr., 14" with crank (Mattel)	3 - 20
M9547 Mousegetars, other designs and years	1 - 12
M9552 Snow White and the Seven Dwarfs xylophone	1 - 12
M9558 Disney On Parade or MMC tambourines	1 - 8
M9562 Magnus electric chord organ	5 - 55
M9563 Misc. Harmonicas, whistles, and plastic instruments	1 - 6

Licensed manufacturers — George Borgfeldt & Co., Inc. (NYC) 1935-39; Carnival Toys, Inc. (Bridgeport, CN then Overland Park, KS) 1973-84; Emenee Industries, Inc. (NYC) 1955-58; Lido Toy Co. (NYC) 1954-55; Mattel, Inc. (LA) 1935-59; Noble & Cooley Co. (Granville, MA) 1935-39, 69-83; Peter Puppet Playthings, Inc. (Brooklyn, NY) 1955-58; Proll Toys, Inc. (Bloomfield, NJ) 1973-84; and Rhythm Band, Inc. (Ft. Worth, TX) 1977-79.

M9600 MUSICAL TOYS

Baby rattles and other baby toys elsewhere listed were among the first musical toys. The plastic toy manufacturers of modern times have produced hundreds of musical toys. The classics in this class, however, are the play pianos made by Marks Brothers.

M9615 Mickey/Minnie grand piano	80 - 800
M9616 Mickey/Minnie animated piano (Marks Bros.)	100 - 1000
M9630 Snow White piano (Marks Bros.)	80 - 800
M9690 Magic Ship musical TV toy (Ideal)	5 - 15

Licensed manufacturers — Ideal Toy Corp. (Hollis, NY) 1968-82; Marks Brothers Co. (Boston, MA) 1934-41; and Spec-Toy-Culars, Inc. (Long Island City, NY) 1957-58, "musical toys".

N1500 NAPKIN RINGS AND HOLDERS

There are several early ceramic napkin rings of undetermined origin. The products of Plastic Novelties and Hutzler are widespread.

N1510 Ceramic	5 - 35
N1520 Mickey, Donald or Snow White (Plastic Novelties), each	5 - 25
N1525 Mickey, Minnie, Donald or Pluto (Hutzler) each	2 - 8

Licensed manufacturers — Hutzler Mfg. Co. (Long Island City, NY) 1947-49 and Plastic Novelties, Inc. (NYC) 1935-55.

N2500 NATIONAL PORCELAIN COMPANY

The National Porcelain Company, Inc. (Trenton, NJ) was a licensee from 1939-42. The 2-1/2" and 3-1/4" figures were produced in white, pastel green, tan and full color. Only the Pinocchio figures are known to the author. Value 5 - 30 each.

N3000 NEWSPAPER COMIC STRIPS

King Features Syndicate, Inc. was licensed to distribute Disney comic strips in 1930 and continues to this date. Mickey Mouse began Jan 13, 1930 (Color Sunday pages Jan 10, 1932). The Donald Duck daily strip started Feb 7, 1938 (Color Sunday pages Dec 10, 1939). These strips continue. Silly Symphonies Sunday color pages ran Jan 10, 1932 and ended on July 12, 1942 shortly after the release of the last Silly Symphony cartoon. Short run color Sunday comics based on feature films began Dec 12, 1937 (Snow White) and ended Dec 16, 1951 with Alice in Wonderland. This series now continues under the title of Treasury of Classic Tales. The Uncle Remus Sunday Color page started Oct 14, 1945 and ran until Dec 31, 1972. A Merry Menagerie black and white panel premiered Jan 13, 1947 and concluded Mar 17, 1962. A True-Life Adventure panel ran Mar 14, 1955 to Apr 14, 1973. An annual Christmas strip began on Nov 28, 1960 and runs each year. Scamp, the son of Lady and the Tramp, began as a color Sunday page Jan 15, 1956 and the daily on Oct 31, 1955. Both continue. A Winnie the Pooh daily and Sunday strips were introduced in 1978.

The first month of the Mickey Mouse strip was written by Walt

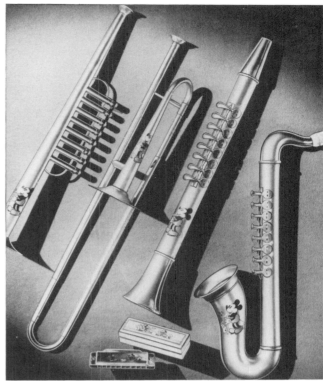

M9509   M9505

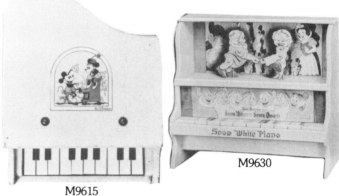

M9630

M9615

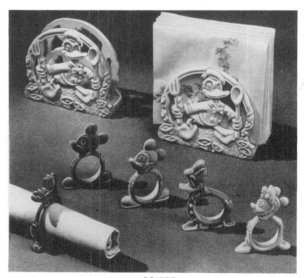

N1525

O5000

O4500

O4501

O4051

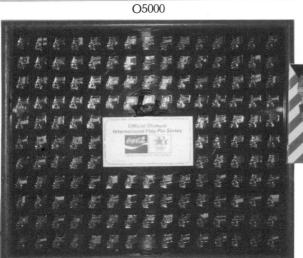

O4013

O4175

P0400

P0420

P0425

Window Pictures. Value 3-10.

Disney and penciled by Ub Iwerks. These are the most valuable b
& w comic strips fetching 4 - 20 each. The Jan 10, 1932 Sunday
page brings 10 - 50. Most others command 1 - 15 for color pages.
Daily strips can be collected for .10 to only a few dollars each for
the oldest material. It's amazing how many old newspapers were
saved. These strips are also available on microfilm at most good
sized libraries and have been reprinted in a number of books.

Also see — ORIGINAL COMIC ART

N6500 NODDERS

A nodder is a figure with its head balanced on a wire axis, hinge
or spring. Tilting the head in one direction, then releasing, triggers
a nodding action.

N6505	Mickey, celluloid	25 - 250
N6510	Donald, celluloid	30 - 300
N6530	Mickey, plastic, 40's	5 - 45
	Alice in Wonderland figures, Tweedle-Dee,	
	Tweedle-Dum, or the Queen of Hearts	See Goebel
N6575	Mickey, Donald or Pluto, papier mache	
	(Brechner), each	2 - 15
N6580	Mickey or Goofy Walt Disney World souvenir	1 - 10

Licensed manufacturers — George Borgfeldt & Co. (NYC) 1930-41; and
Dan Brechner & Co., Inc. (NYC) 1961-63.

O4000 OLYMPICS

Sam the Olympic Eagle was created by Disney artist Bob
Moore and presented to the Los Angeles Olympic Organizing
Committee. Sam became the mascot of the 1984 Summer Olym-
pics and was copyrighted by the committee in 1980. Disney makes
no claim to the character, yet his resemblance to Sam the Eagle in
Disneyland's "America Sings" is unmistakable. The Olympic Eagle
is shorter, has larger eyes and beak, plus the Olympic logo on his
hat band. Goofy was adopted as the mascot of the 1980 French
Olympic team in remembrance of the character's many sports
cartoons. Thus was born Sport Goofy. He was promoted exten-
sively during the 1984 Olympic year. Disneyland also promoted a
special Olympic metal admission ticket and special events at the
park. Sponsor pins became a new collecting field in themselves.
The amount of merchandise and promotion pieces was stagger-
ing, but the following sample is representative.

O4010	First series of Sam event pins, framed	100 - 400
O4011	Second series of Sam event pins, framed	75 - 350
O4012	Third series of Sam event pins, framed	50 - 300
O4013	Coca-Cola 150 flag pin series, framed	10 - 150

All sponsor pin sets have gone way up and have come way
down in price. Many counterfeits have been produced. Collectors
should beware.

O4050	Official program	1 - 5
O4051	Youth handbook	1 - 4
O4075	Mugs, plates, or bowls, each	1 - 4
O4100	Rings	1 - 8
O4110	Jewelry	2 - 15
O4150	Posters with Sam	1 - 4
O4175	Playing cards	1 - 4
O4200	Baseball type hats	1 - 4
O4500	Disneyland Olympic metal ticket, each	5 - 25
O4501	Disneyland Olympic night program	1 - 5

O5000 ORIGINAL COMIC ART

Black and white art for comic books, newspaper daily and
Sunday strips, plus art done for non-film promotional or licensee
purposes has been sold over the years. A run of the mill daily strip
may bring as little as 15 - 25 whereas a Sunday or comic book page
by a collected artist may command several hundred. Comic art, in
general, has never reached the level of animation drawings and
cels. Original work of Carl Barks is the lone exception. Here again
is an area where each individual piece must be judged on its own
merit.

P0400 PAINT BOXES AND SETS

There is overlap between paint, crayon and drawing sets. Products listed here are ones where paints of some type were the
dominant factor — metal box of water colors, water color paint
sets, paint by numbers, magic water paints, etc. Marks Brothers

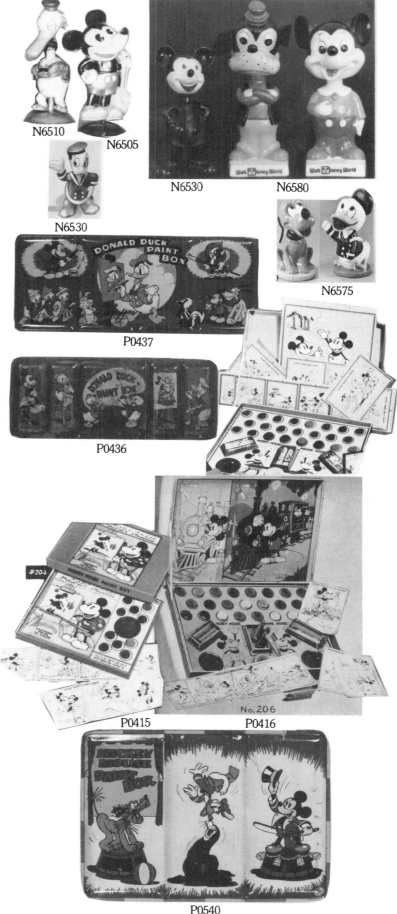

N6510

N6505

N6530

N6530

N6580

N6575

P0437

P0436

P0415

P0416

No. 206

P0540

P0435

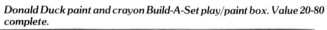

Donald Duck paint and crayon Build-A-Set play/paint box. Value 20-80 complete.

P0440

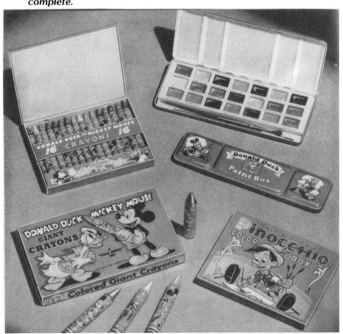

P0430

P0440

first produced such sets in 1934. Transogram has probably been the largest producer over the years. Page of London water color sets are widely distributed in the U. S.; imported by F. J. Stanton Co., Inc. (NYC).

P0415	Mickey Mouse paint set #204 (Marks Bros.)	15 - 90
P0416	Mickey Mouse paint set #206 (Marks Bros.)	25 - 110
P0417	Mickey Mouse easel paint set # 254 (Marks Bros.)	35 - 175
P0420	Donald Duck paint set (Whitman) 1936	25 - 250
P0425	Walt Disney Character Paint Set (Standard Toykraft)	10 - 50
P0430	Pinocchio Color Box (Transogram) 1940	8 - 35
P0435	Mickey Mouse Paint Box (Transogram)	5 - 25
P0436	Donald Duck Paint Box (Transogram) 8 colors	5 - 20
P0437	Donald Duck Paint Box (Transogram) 21 colors	5 - 25
P0440	Donald Duck Paint Sets (Transogram) in paperboard boxes (3 sizes)	8 - 60
P0450	Mickey Mouse Paint Box (space suits) (Transogram)	4 - 20
P0460	MagicPaint pictures (paint with water) (Artcraft), each	1 - 8
P0490	Spray and Play air brush set (Ideal)	1 - 10
P0500	Jungle Book paint and crayon set (Hasbro)	1 - 10
P0540	Page sets vary dramatically from 8 color to 48 color and perhaps larger. There are no U. S. records to show the years of license, but paint boxes found indicate a period of at least 20 years. Smaller and more recent boxes (listing Strauss as distribution) are valued 1 - 5. Larger and older ones with 40's style drawings are valued at	2 - 25.

Licensed manufacturers — Artcraft Paper Products (Cincinnati, OH) 1955-56; Cadillac Toy Mfg. Co. (Bronx, NY) 1953-54; Hasbro Industries, Inc. division of Empire Pencil Co. (Pawtucket, RI) 1970-84; Ideal Toy Corp. (Hollis, NY) 1968-82; Marks Brothers Co. (Boston, MA) 1934-41, 46-48; D. A. Pachter Co. (Chicago) 1943-45; Standard Toykraft Products (Brooklyn, NY) 1939-41; Transogram Co., Inc. (NYC) 1939-42, 45-55, 68-71; and Whitman Publishing Co. (Racine, WI) 1933-85.

1934 Marks Brother Ad

P0430   P0450

P0460

P0500

P0490

P0540

Disney Subjects are available on two groups of Dennison's merchandise:

1, Gift Dressings, including wrapping papers and printed Cellophane, seals, cards, and tags for Everyday and for Christmas; 2, Table Decorations, including Party Packages, table covers, napkins, and nut cups for Everyday, Christmas, and Hallowe'en.

The designs vary with each season and for each holiday. Consult your Dennison salesman or nearest Dennison office for particulars.

DENNISON MANUFACTURING CO.
Licensee
FRAMINGHAM, MASS.

New York Salesrooms   220 Fifth Avenue

PC623

P0624

P0612

P0610

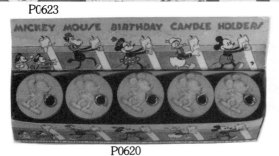

P0620

P0651

P0650

P0624

Party hats circa '50's; perhaps Great Lakes Press. Value 2-7 each.

P0600 PARTY SUPPLIES AND HATS

Mickey Mouse has been the theme of birthday parties since the early 30's. Other Disney characters have been in the spotlight, too. Party favors, baskets, cake decorations, noisemakers, napkins, nut cups, paper plates and cups are included in this class.

P0610	Borgfeldt paper horn 7"	8 - 55
P0611	Same as P0610, but 12"	10 - 75
P0612	Same as P0610, but with wooden handle	9 - 65
P0620	Candles or candle holders, each pack (Cypress)	5 - 20
P0623	Paper party sets (includes napkins, printed crepe papers, decorations, table cover and doilies (Dennison) 30's, sets	25 - 250
P0623	Parts of Dennison party sets, each	3 - 20
P0624	Main character and Snow White party goods (Adler) each	5 - 25
P0625	Pinocchio character center pieces, (Palmer-Weller), each	5 - 35
P0626	Pinocchio favors (Palmer-Weller)	3 - 15
P0635	Cake "Decostrips" (Seagren), each	3 - 15
P0639	Mickey Chicago Herald-American doilies, each	3 - 10
P0640	Paper party kits (Great Lakes)	15 - 85
P0650	Best Plastics candle holder set, boxed	8 - 20
P0651	Best Plastics party baskets (3) on card	8 - 20
P0655	Centerpieces 50's and 60's	1 - 15
P0657	Davy Crockett napkins (Beach)	2 - 15
P0675	Hallmark party kits	3 - 25

Licensed manufacturers — Adler Favor & Novelty Co., Inc. (St. Louis, MO) 1938-41; American Merri-Lei Corp. (NYC) 1934-35; Bochmann Brothers, Inc. (Philadelphia, PA) 1935-36, 57-58; Best Plastics Corp. (Brooklyn, NY) 1955-57; Beach Products, Inc. (Kalamazoo, MI) 1955, 68-83; George Borgfeldt & Co. (NYC) 1930-50; Carousel Party Favors, Inc. (No. Hollywood, CA) 1979-84; Cypress Novelty Corp. (Brooklyn, NY) 1936-38; Dennison Mfg. Co. (NYC) 1933-36, 62-65; Great Lakes Press Corp aka Rendoll Paper Corp. (Rochester, NY) 1950-55; Hallmark Cards, Inc. (Kansas City, MO) 1972-84; Seagren Products, Inc. (Brooklyn, NY) 1946-48; and Palmer-Weller Co. (NYC) 1940-41.

P0625   P0626

P0800 PATCHES AND LABELS

Makers of illustrated character labels for clothing plus uniform and souvenir patches are listed at this class.

P0810	Clothing labels, 30's and 40's, each	1 - 10
P0811	Clothing labels, 50's-present	1 - 7
P0820	Uniform patches, each	2 - 14
P0825	Mickey Mouse Club patches (Bostonian)	1 - 12
P0830	Special event patches, theme park, each	2 - 18
P0840	Souvenir patches, theme park, each	1 - 5
P0860	Plastic label makers (Rotex), each	1 - 3

Licensed manufacturers — Bostonian Process Co. (Hackensack, NJ) 1955-56; Clover Embroidered Trimmings, Inc. (NYC) 1975-83; International Rotex, Inc. (Reno, NV) 1982-84; Penn Emblem Co. (Philadelphia, PA) 1979-81; National Woven Label Co. (NYC) 1939-41; and Whitney Mfg. Co. (NYC) 1938-41.

P0635

P0810

P0675

P0639

P0820

P0830

P0810

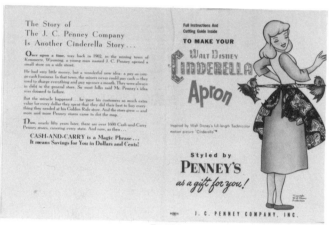

P0926

P0950

P0915

P1030

P1060

P0900 PATTERNS

When the demand for the original Mickey Mouse doll overwhelmed supply, Disney authorized the McCall Company to duplicate Charlotte Clark's doll pattern. In addition to patterns for other dolls, ones for aprons, costumes, clothing, and character doll clothes have been licensed. Transfers for these patterns and other uses were sometimes sold separately.

P0901	Charlotte Clark McCall pattern (used to make Mickey or Minnie dolls in 3 sizes)	20 - 150
P0903	McCall Kaumagraph transfer #90	5 - 25
P0906	McCall Kaumagraph transfer #796	4 - 20
P0915	McCall Snow White doll dress pattern	4 - 20
P0918	Snow White frock (Wrigley)	6 - 30
P0920	Simplicity doll pattern	8 - 50
P0921	Simplicity embroidery/applique transfers, Mickey, Minnie or Pluto, each	3 - 18
P0926	Cinderella apron pattern (Penney's)	2 - 10
P0950	Mary Poppins doll pattern (McCall's)	3 - 15

Licensed manufacturers — McCall Co. (NYC) 1932-45, 54-59, 64-65; J. C. Penney Co. (Pittsburgh, PA) 1950; Simplicity Pattern Co., Inc. (NYC) 1944-46; and William Wrigley, Jr. Co. (Chicago) 1938-39, Doublemint Gum offer.

P1000 PENCIL SHARPENERS

There were early celluloid figural pencil sharpeners, but usually the first image that comes to mind when Disney pencil sharpeners are mentioned is some product of Plastic Novelties (1935-55). There have been wall or desk mount units and many other "pencil box" sharpeners as well.

P1005	Mickey, figural celluloid	20 - 100
P1008	Donald, figural celluloid	20 - 100
P1020	Plastic Novelties, figural sharpeners — Mickey, Donald, Snow White, Dopey, Pinocchio, Lampwick, Jiminy Cricket, Figaro, Ferdinand or Dumbo, each	5 - 20
P1030	Plastic Novelties, rectangular sharpeners, same characters as P1020, each	4 - 16
P1040	Plastic Novelties, circular sharpeners, same characters as P1020, each	4 - 16
P1050	Same as 1040, but with brass frame, each	4 - 16
P1060	Plastic Novelties, circular with convoluted edge, Mickey, Pluto, Goofy, Donald, Joe Carioca, Panchito, Br'er Rabbit, Br'er Fox, Br'er Bear, Casey, Peter (and the Wolf), Hep Cats and Baby Hep, each	3 - 15

Licensed manufacturers — Apsco Products, Inc. (LA) 1960-64; George Borgfeldt & Co. (NYC) 1930-50; and Plastic Novelties, Inc. (NYC) 1935-55.

P1200 PENNANTS

Felt pennants were sold in conjunction with the 1948 Ice Capades show and perhaps earlier. Disneyland, the Mickey Mouse Club, events and other theme parks and "lands" have been subjects of individual pennants.

P1220	Ice Capades	4 - 24
P1230	Disneyland (various colors), each	3 - 10
P1240	Mickey Mouse Club (various sizes and colors), each	2 - 16
P1260	Fort Wilderness	1 - 8
P1270	Main Street, Adventureland, Frontierland, Fantasyland, or Tomorrowland, each	1 - 4
P1280	EPCOT Center (Figment and Dreamfinder, Future World, or World Showcase), each	1 - 3

P1300 PENS, PENCILS AND PENCIL BOXES

The Inkograph Company made pens and pencils starting in 1935 after the Joseph Dixon Crucible Co. set the pace with a broad line of pencil boxes beginning in 1931. Dixon also made wooden and color pencils for "sketching, drawing, and map coloring." Ingersoll sold ballpoint pens with watches and rings in the late 40's. Hasbro was the major maker in the late 40's and 50's; and from 1968-84.

P1305	Mickey Ink-D-Cator fountain pen (Inkograph)	10 - 85
P1306	Mickey fountain pen (Inkograph) not made w/Mickey's head like others	5 - 50

P0921

P0903

P1005

P1008

P1020

ICE CAPADES

P1220

MICKEY MOUSE

P1401

Disneyland

P1230

MEMBER
MICKEY MOUSE
CLUB

MOUSEKETEERS

P1240

P1401

Walt Disney World

AMERICA ON PARADE

P1270

DONALD DUCK Pencil Case

P1420

Walt Disney World

FORT WILDERNESS

P1260

MICKEY'S

Disneyland

F2090

Ingersoll

P1325

P1405   P1310

P1307	Inkograph mechanical pencil	5 - 50
P1308	Inkograph pen holder and point (fountain feed pen)	4 - 35
P1310	Dixon wooden lead pencil	5 - 50
P1311	Dixon colored pencil set (2 versions), each	5 - 45
P1325	Ingersoll Mickey or Donald ball point pen	3 - 20
P1400	Dixon pencil box (no drawer)	5 - 25
P1401	Dixon pencil box (one drawer)	6 - 35
P1402	Dixon pencil box (two drawers)	7 - 40
P1405	Dixon figural pencil box, Mickey (2 versions), Minnie or Red Riding Hood, each	10 - 80
P1410	Dixon military insignia pencil box	6 - 55
P1411	Mickey ball point pen (Charmore)	10 - 70
P1420	Hasbro pencil boxes, each	4 - 20
P1421	Hasbro pencils, each	1 - 10
P1445	Empire pencil boxes or cases	3 - 12
P1449	Hasbro since 1968	1 - 9

Licensed manufacturers — The Charmore Co. (NYC) 1947; Commonwealth Toy and Novelty Co. (NYC) 1938-40, 70-72; Joseph Dixon Crucible Co. (Jersey City, NJ) 1931-42; Empire Pencil Co. (Shelbyville, TN) 1968-71; Faber-Castell Corp. (Newark, NJ) 1975-84, pens, pencils, markers, colored pencils; Hasbro/Hassenfeld Brothers, Inc. (Pawtucket, RI) 1949-55, 68-84; Ingersoll (see U. S. Time); Inkograph Co., Inc. (NYC) 1935-38; Russ Berrie & Co. (Oakland, NJ) 1975-76, pens; Sheaffer Eaton division of Texton Corp. (Pittsfield, MA) 1982-84, Kaleidoscope ball point pen and rolling ball pens; United States Time Corp. (NYC) 1945-71.

P1310

P1400

P1305   P1306

P1400

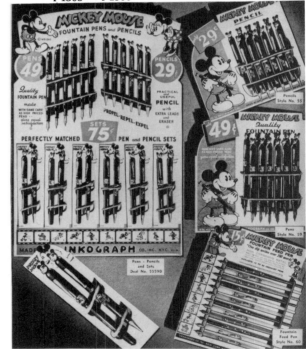

P1307   P1308

P1411

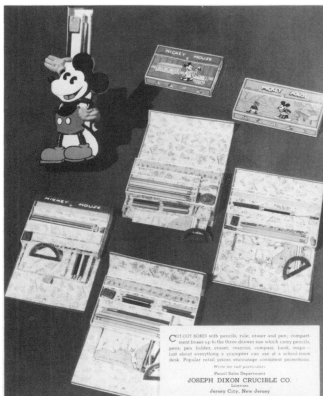

CUT-OUT BOXES with pencils, rule, eraser and pen; compartment boxes up to the three-drawer size which carry pencils, pens, pen holder, eraser, crayons, compass, bank, map—just about everything a youngster can use at a school-room desk. Popular retail prices encourage consistent promotions.

Write for full particulars

Pencil Sales Department

JOSEPH DIXON CRUCIBLE CO.

Licensee

Jersey City, New Jersey

P1400

P1401

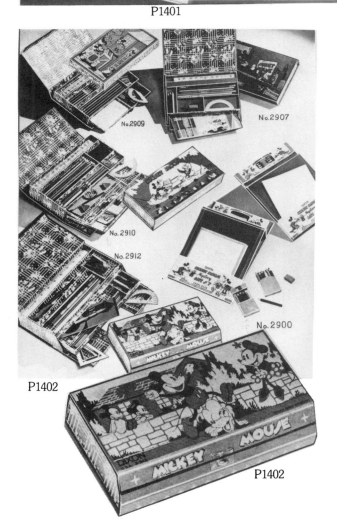

No.2909

No.2907

No.2910

No.2912

No.2900

P1402

P1402

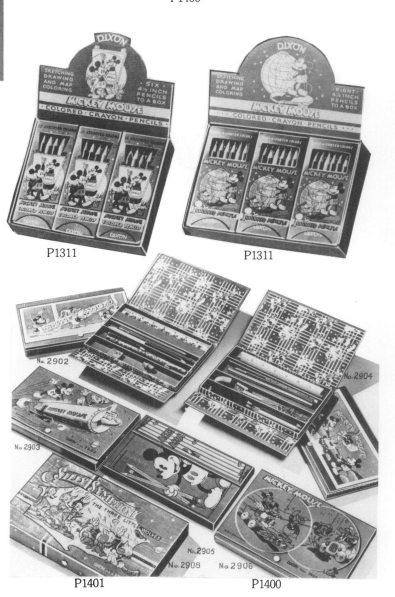

P1311

P1311

No.2902

No.2904

No.2903

No.2905

No.2908

No.2906

P1401

P1400

P1400

P1402

P1402

P1401

P1421

P1410

P1420

P1420

P1445

141

P1500 PERFUME, COSMETICS AND TOILETRIES

Perfume and other children's toiletries (except soap) didn't arrive until the time of Snow White. The Russian made set of Seven Dwarf figural perfume bottles has been made for many years, but probably doesn't date back to the film's original release. Similar Mickey, Donald and Pluto figural bottles are of unknown origin.

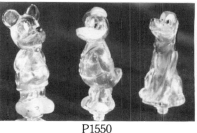

P1550   P1580

P1530	Snow White perfume bottle in card	8 - 85
P1540	Seven Dwarf set (Russian)	10 - 70
P1550	Mickey, Donald or Pluto perfume bottles, each	5 - 15
P1580	Disney Dollies (Ben Rickert)	1 - 2

Licensed manufacturers — DEP Corp. (LA) 1974-77; Flora Tallinn (name on Russian perfume bottles) made as late as the 70's; The Lander Company, Inc. (NYC) 1938-40; M. R. Nadel Co. (NYC) 1970-71; Oculens, Ltd. (Oceanside, NY) 1976-83; and Ben Rickert, Inc. (Wayne, NJ) 1980-84.

B1900 PINBACK BUTTONS & BADGES

In 1927 Oswald the Lucky Rabbit was the first Disney character to appear on a pinback button. The first Mickey Mouse Club got off the ground in 1929 and was the subject of pinback buttons for several years. Newspaper comic strips, advertising sponsor buttons, and Kay Kamen giveaways were the prime subjects during the 30's. There were a number of buttons and tabs for the TV Mickey Mouse Club in the 50's and a few theme park buttons in the 50's-60's period. By the time Walt Disney productions celebrated its 50th year in 1973, pinback buttons had become a part of every promotion — Grad Nite, America on Parade, Mickey and Donald's 50th birthdays, The Disney Channel, new theme parks, park souvenir buttons, film buttons, and the much sought after Walt Disney World Costuming Division buttons. Collecting post 1980 buttons has achieved mania proportions on the West Coast. Over 150 fake buttons have been made photographically or otherwise created in violation of Disney copyrights. Prices commanded by authentic buttons only years old have been totally out of line with the eventual selling price when availability became known. The Disney organization has obliged collectors by issuing buttons in conjunction with every occasion, film, or promotional event.

P1540

P1901	Oswald the Lucky Rabbit	25 - 250
P1902	Mickey Mouse Club button	15 - 85
P1903	Sears Mickey Mouse Club buttons	15 - 60
P1904	Theater Mickey Mouse Club buttons, same as P1902, but with names of various theaters, each	15 - 85
P1905	Mickey Mouse Club button (waving)	10 - 60
P1906	Same as P1905 but with theater name, each	10 - 65
P1915	Mickey Mouse Club button (orange)	15 - 75
P1920	Fox Broadway MMC button	25 - 140
P1921	Fox California MMC button	25 - 140
P1922	Mickey Mouse Club (black on white)	15 - 50
P1925	RKO Kiddie Kartoon Klub	40 - 100
P1928	Mickey Mouse Club officer buttons	Value ?
P1934	Western Theater Mickey Mouse	25 - 55
P1935	St. Louis Button Mickey Mouse 3/4"	25 - 50
P1936	Mickey Mouse (standing)	15 - 50
P1937	Mickey Mouse (walk and wave)	15 - 80
P1938	Mickey Mouse, full color	40 - 75
P1940	Police Department, Fire Department or Aviation Department badges, each	50 - 250
P1945	Milk promotion buttons, cloth with brass rim, Mickey (crude), Mickey (classic) different color backgrounds, Big Bad Wolf, Pigs, each	8 - 40
P1955	"For Better Health" milk button	25 - 250
P1956	Southern Dairies Ice Cream	20 - 200
P1960	Spingle-Bell-Chicko-K	20 - 90
P1963	Mickey Mouse Shoes tab (Truitt Bros.)	8 - 50
P1964	Mickey Mouse Undies	15 - 35
P1965	Mickey Mouse Hose	16 - 50
P1966	Penney's Back-to-School	10 - 32
P1967	Mickey Mouse Sneakers (Converse)	35 - 350
P1968	Mickey Mouse Soap	35 - 300
P1969	Mickey Mouse Emerson Radio	15 - 60
P1974	7th Birthday of Mickey Mouse (1935)	20 - 100
P1975	Mickey Santa at Merkel's Toyland	25 - 250
P1976	Donald Duck Jackets	30 - 180

P1940

P2051   P2043

P1977	Donald Duck Jellies	35 - 200
P1978	Icy-Frost Twins or Ducky Dubble member	20 - 100
P1980	Mickey Mouse Good Teeth	15 - 60
P1981	Mickey on Skis (gloves and mittens)	20 - 75
P1985	Mickey mouse Globe Trotter and Follow My Adventures, buttons, various bakeries and dairies, each	15 - 35
P2010	Los Angeles Evening Herald and Express	15 - 45
P2011	Sunday Herald and Examiner	18 - 80
P2012	Mickey Mouse Evening Ledger Comics	10 - 100
P2013	Minnie Mouse Evening Ledger Comics	10 - 120
P2014	The Atlanta Georgian's Silver Anniversary (1937)	30 - 100
P2015	Boston Sunday Advertiser	15 - 55
P2025	Mickey Mouse (Kay Kamen)	17 - 75
P2026	Who's Afraid of the Big Bad Wolf (Kamen)	18 - 80
P2027	Donald Duck Wanna Fight (Kamen)	50 - 250
P2030	Snow White Jingle Club member	5 - 30
P2031	Snow White Jingle Club 3"	17 - 75
P2040	Walt Disney's Pinocchio	10 - 40
P2041	Pinocchio Good Teeth	30 - 120
P2042	Pinocchio on Victor Records	35 - 175
P2043	Jiminy Cricket Official Conscience Medal	15 - 60
P2045	Jiminy Cricket United Way	5 - 30
P2050	Dumbo D-X	15 - 40
P2051	Dumbo song book	30 - 100
P2064	Mickey Mouse camera tab	15 - 50

P1900 PINBACK BUTTONS, BADGES & TABS continue in Volume Three of *Tomart's Illustrated DISNEYANA Catalog and Price Guide.*